"The Good Soldier", a Selection of Soldiers Letters

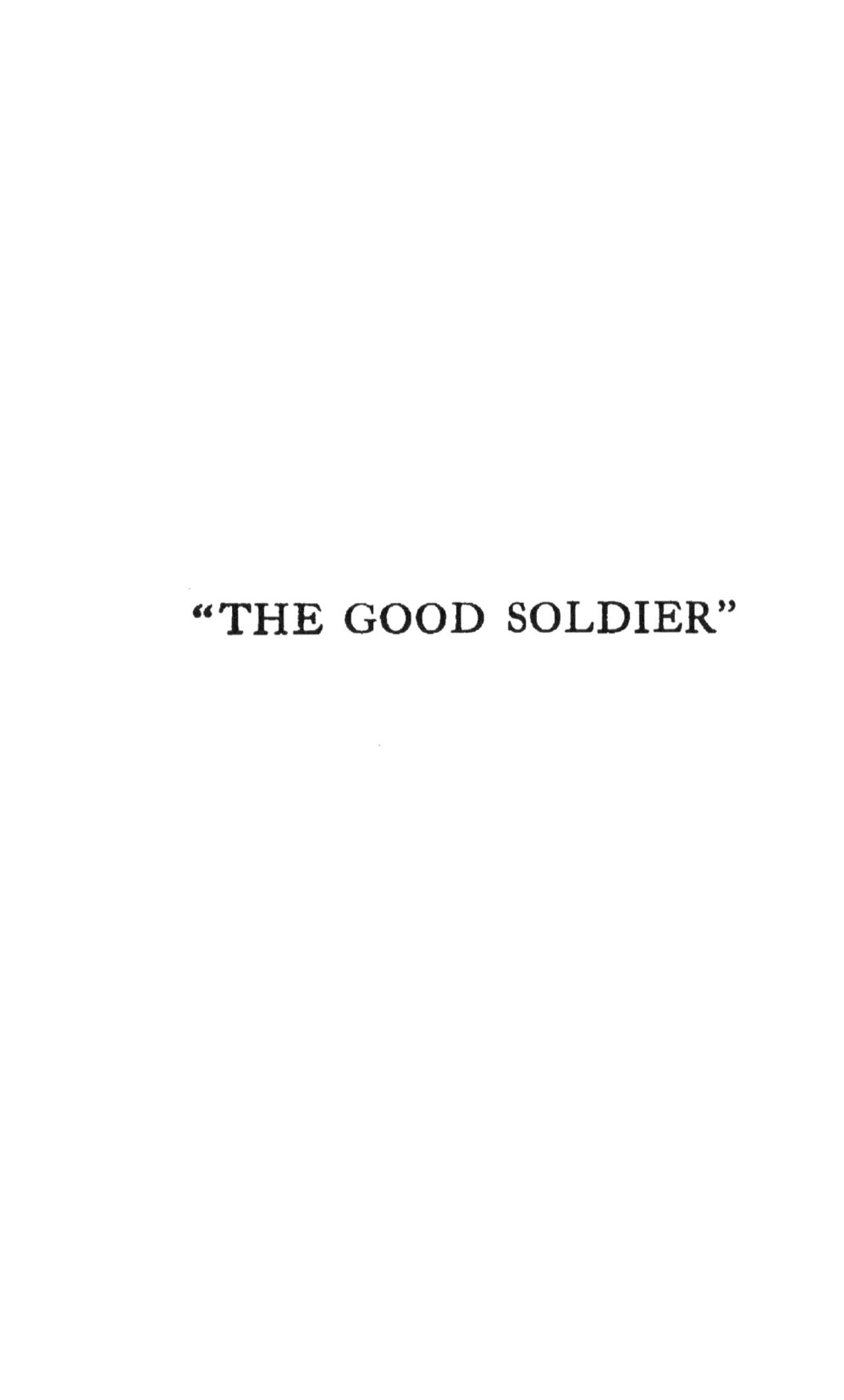

"THE GOOD SOLDIER"

THE MACMILLAN COMPANY
NEW YORK · BOSTON · CHICAGO · DALLAS
ATLANTA · SAN FRANCISCO

MACMILLAN & CO., Limited
LONDON · BOMBAY · CALCUTTA
MELBOURNE

THE MACMILLAN CO. OF CANADA, Ltd.
TORONTO

"THE GOOD SOLDIER"

A SELECTION OF SOLDIERS' LETTERS, 1914-1918

WITH COMMENT BY
N P. DAWSON

New York
THE MACMILLAN COMPANY
1918

All rights reserved

Whither they mirthfully hastened as jostling for honor,
Not since her birth has our Earth seen such worth loosed upon her.

— RUDYARD KIPLING.

INTRODUCTION

HERE are boys, all sorts of boys: French, English Italian, American; young artists, budding novelists and poets; musicians; drab and spectacled London office clerks just off a stool; an auctioneer from Brixton; elderly married men, as old as thirty-five, and " little nephews " of sixteen; Catholics, Protestants, Christians, Jews; grave young students in arms; Crusaders of France; Oxford and Cambridge men and French schoolboys; American college men and American rich men's sons from New York and California; a ball-player from Kentucky; " those splendid Canadians "; favorites of fortune and widows' sons; French prisoners in Germany, and German prisoners in France, and little Antonio in Austria looking longingly out across the sea to Italy; aviators, ambulance drivers, truck drivers, stretcher-bearers, gunners; plucky British officers willing to " bear the blunt "; and dashing young Saint-Cyriens going into battle in white gloves and plume — the " élite of the world," the new aristocracy, not waiting to see or be summoned, but, at the first call to arms, rushing forth, as Kipling writes, " as jostling for honor."

These are soldiers' letters written home. But reading, one finds that he does not think of them as letters at all, but as boys: Enzo, Antonio, Robert, Arthur, Gaston, William, Marcel, Harry, Victor. And one is filled with pity that they are boys, " mere men " as more than one of them says, pitted against professional soldiers, experts in the refined arts of modern war. But if one thing more than another is revealed in the letters, it is that the writers do not want to be pitied; rather envied. One boy tells his parents (an American, by his speech) not, with their worrying, to " take the edge off " from his own complete contentment with what he is doing. A French boy says not to call him " poor Jean "; rather to say " dear Jean " or " brave Jean " or even " little Jean," but not " poor Jean." All express in one way and another that death has no terrors for " the good soldier."

Never probably in the history of the world have so many letters been written as during the great war. At the front, it is said that the most important order of the day is not a trench raid, a gas attack, or a big bombardment, but, first, food, and next the mail. At home, the mail would probably be put first. Many of the letters reveal not only an unexpected literary talent, since most of the writers are very young, but invariably a wonderful spirit: the spirit of " the good soldier " quick to resent injustice and wrong, eager to fight for what he believes is right, and willing to die for it, too.

No one can read the letters of these glorious boys and not resent the belittling assumption that all the fighting men are dumb victims of a " capitalistic " war, driven against their will. Nor can one believe

INTRODUCTION

it is adventure alone calling to youth. A few, here and there, to be sure, may have been like the "little nephew," the sixteen-year-old French boy, who thought the firing and the guns especially arranged to "please me!" But almost without exception, no matter in what spirit they entered the war, once in it, they become gravely conscious of its great issues, and are determined not only to do their bit, but their all, and see it through.

Some of the boys fight for Mamma; others for grandmother (this means Alsace); others fight, with the bayonet, to avenge the honor of the "French women, our sisters." Some rush to the assault shouting "Savoia"; others "Vive la France!" But all are only varying expressions of the same thing. There is unanimity of opinion, no matter what the language, that they are engaged in a war against war itself; a war for freedom and justice not only for one's own country but for every one; a war, as one young Italian poetically puts it, against those who would "kill the light."

In every collection of letters that has been published, among much that is personal and boyish — and at times is manifestly the supreme literary effort of a young life — there is generally one letter more sober than the rest, and serious beyond the years of the writer. Such a letter is not necessarily a conscious "last word" (boys do not like a fuss), but something written in a more solemn mood, perhaps dimly prescient. These letters are most often addressed to mothers, and, oddly enough, endeavor to give rather than to seek comfort. "These are the days when men should be born without mothers," one writes; but another says more truly that, on the contrary, these are the days when mothers should be proud, as Spartan mothers.

On the battle line, it is said a soldier derives comfort and courage from contact with his fellows, the touch of shoulder and elbow. In the same manner, it has seemed that some of these letters should be brought in a volume together. They belong together. The enemy may extend its empire over the world, sweep it from sea to sea, but the spirit of these letters cannot be defeated. The dead will rise again.

N. P. D.

CONTENTS

	PAGE
ENZO VALENTINI	1
AN ANONYMOUS SOLDIER	5
ANTONIO	9
ROBERT LE ROUX	12
GASTON RIOU	16
A GERMAN PRISONER IN FRANCE	20
ARTHUR GEORGE HEATH	22
OBSEVER B—— DE P——	27
"GOD PUNISH ENGLAND!"	30
PIERRE-MAURICE MASSON	33
CONINGSBY DAWSON	38
A SAINT-CYRIEN	41
ROBERT ERNEST VERNÈDE	45
ANDRÉ CORNET-AUQUIER	49
MARCEL ETEVE	52
THE SOLDIER PRIEST	56
ROBERT HERTZ	62
DECORATED	65
ALAN SEEGER	67
DIXON SCOTT	70

CONTENTS

	PAGE
FERDINAND BELMONT	73
"ONE YOUNG MAN"	77
ALEXANDER DOUGLAS GILLESPIE	79
HARRY BUTTERS	83
"A TEMPORARY GENTLEMAN"	87
NORMAN PRINCE	90
VICTOR CHAPMAN	93
ALFRED EUGÉNE CASALIS	97
"R. A. L.," CANADIAN STRETCHER-BEARER	100
"MY LITTLE NEPHEW"	104
JEAN RIVAL	106
LESLIE BUSWELL	108
WILLIAM YORKE STEVENSON	110
"CAMION LETTERS"	114
A FRENCH MRS. BIXBY	117
A LITTLE MOTHER	118
JEAN GIRAUDOUX	121
YVONNE X——	124
CHARLES PÉGUY	127
LOUIS KEENE	130
CAPTAIN GILBERT NOBBS	133
WOUNDED	137
HUMPHREY COBB	140
EDMUND YERBURY PRIESTMAN	143
THE MARSEILLAISE	148
DONALD HANKEY	150

CONTENTS

	PAGE
A French Schoolboy	152
William M. Barber	154
Vive L'Alsace!	157
Maurice Génevoix	159
R. Derby Holmes	161
Alexander McClintock	163
Robert Reaser	165
Arthur Guy Empey	168
"The Good Soldier"	171
"Pages Actuelles"	173
A. Letter of a French Mother	173
B. Letter of an American Mother	173
C. Farewell of a French Soldier	174
D. Farewell of an American Soldier	175
Poem "Lament," by Wilfrid Gibson	177

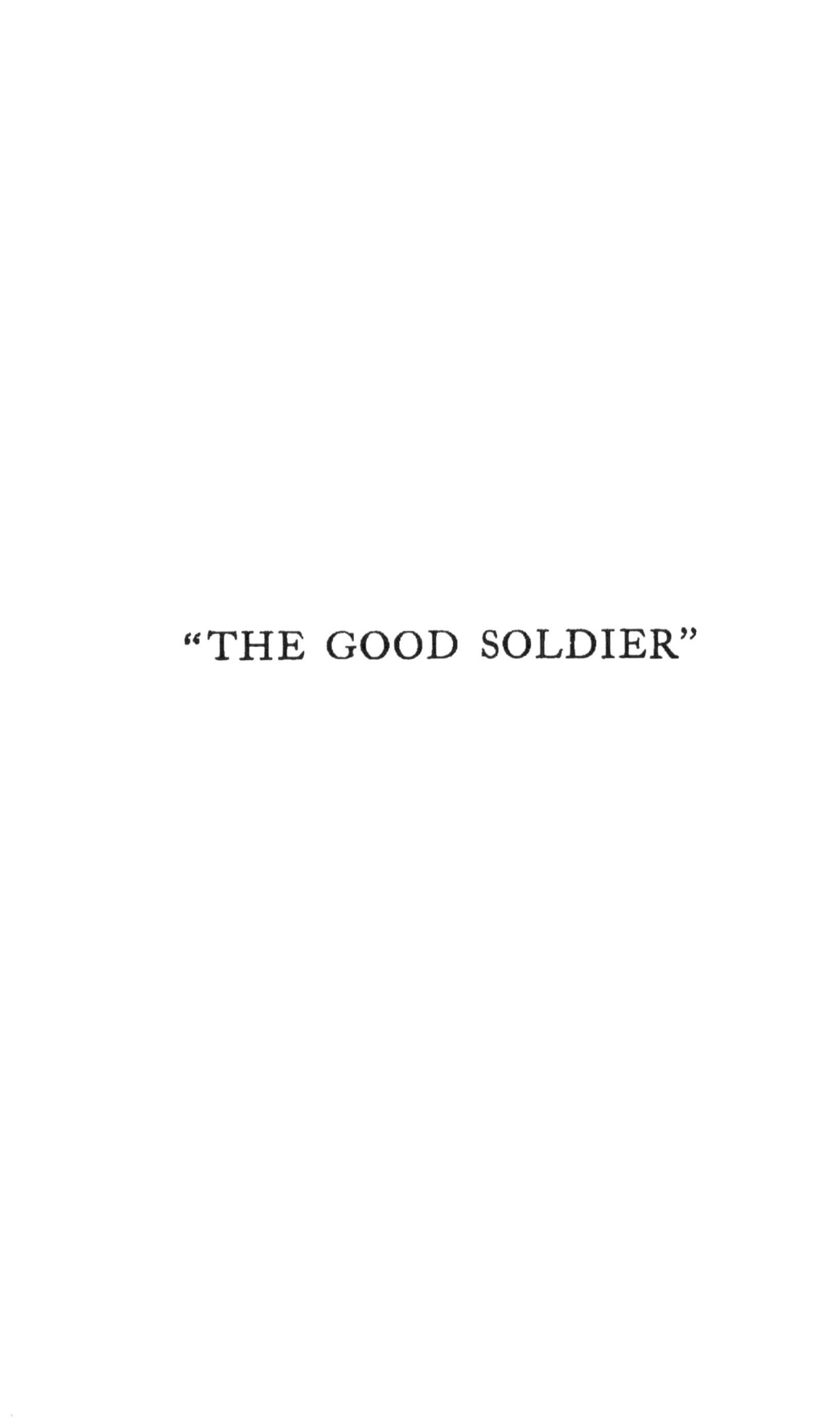

"THE GOOD SOLDIER"

"THE GOOD SOLDIER"

ENZO VALENTINI

It must be that some of the ecstasy and beautiful and poetic spirit of St. Francis of Assisi entered into a boy of the neighboring hill-top town of Perugia. Enzo Valentini was the son of Count Valentini, mayor of Perugia. He was a student of the College of Perugia, and was rarely gifted. A lover of poetry and the natural sciences, he read Fabre and Maeterlinck. He was also an artist. One of his last etchings showing some trees, he called "The Survivors"— not realizing that in Belgium and France not even the trees survive.

Upon Italy's declaration of war in May, 1915, Enzo Valentini enlisted as a private. He was unwilling to wait for anything else to be arranged. He was eighteen. He immediately entered into the life of the barracks. He refused to return home at night as he would have been permitted to do. His one passionate desire was to "train my body and elevate my soul for the great sacrifice."

After he had been two days in the barracks, he wrote to his aunt: " Barracks life has transformed me. In two days I have become accustomed to everything: to sleep on straw between two double-bass performers, to wash the mess tins, to drill and handle the gun. I have become accustomed to the most heterogeneous company and to the greatest assortment of smells a susceptible nose could possibly imagine. Moreover, now that I have adapted myself to it, the military life suits me very well. The vin ordinaire is excellent, for example. The bread is also very good; cut into thin small pieces and swimming in the tin, it reminds me of pigeon soup. The pigeon is lacking, but I imagine it so well that the effect is the same. In the same way, I imagine that the coffee is well sweetened, that the half empty straw mattress serving me as a couch is a bed of down, and more of the same sort. Imagination makes me happy, aided by enthusiasm that has become my regular disposition instead of an occasional and foolish exhilaration. Your letter has given me the greatest pleasure; one sees with how much love you accompany me. But your compliments are exaggerated. I deserve no credit for what I have done. It is the joy of my soul that I have translated into acts, and not the melancholy product of my brain. Soon I shall be writing you from the front."

When two months have passed since " dead with fatigue and drunk with joy," he arrived at the front, he writes to his mother that it seems as if it were only yesterday, and that searching his conscience, he finds that he has lost nothing, unless it is little meannesses and cowardices, while he has gained inestimable spiritual treasures. He is sure that he has discovered the secret of happiness. " I am happy, little mother, and I think that I have found the secret of being happy always." He tells her not to worry for fear he will rush into any foolish "heroisms." He says: "That would be wrong, because it would consume the energy that should be saved for the moment of the ultimate sacrifice."

He left Perugia in July. He never returned. In less than three months he was killed. In the attack in which he lost his life, it is said he was the first out of the trench. Arriving at an advanced position, he and one of his comrades embraced each other. He showed his friend his cap in which he had put a sprig of edelweiss. He said when he jumped out of the trench, he saw it at his feet. "Isn't it pretty?" he asked. "It will bring me luck." Then shouting "Italia! Savoia!" he went on. He was hit by five bullets.

Before departing for the front, Enzo Valentini made his will and testament, to be opened only in the case of his death, the last poetic words of which are: "Be strong, little mother. From beyond, he sends to you his farewell, to papa, to his brothers, to all who have loved him — your son who has given his body to fight against those who would kill the light."

(Letter of Enzo Valentini)

Little mother, in several days I am going to depart for the front. I am writing my farewell to you, which you are to read only if I die. Let it also be my farewell to papa, to my brothers, to all those who have cared for me in this world.

Since on earth my heart, in its love and recognition, has always to you given its best thoughts, it is to you also that I wish to make known my last wishes. . . .

Try, if you can, not to weep for me too much. Think that even if I do not return, I am not for that reason dead. It, my body, the inferior part of me, may suffer and die, but not I. I, the soul, cannot die, because I come from God and must return to God. I was born for happiness, and through the happiness that is at the bottom of all suffering, I am to return into everlasting joy. If at times I have been the prisoner of my body, it has not been for always. My death is a liberation, the beginning of the true life, the return to the Infinite. Therefore, do not weep for me. If you think of the immortal beauty of the Ideas for which my soul has desired to sacrifice my body, you will not weep. But if your mother's heart mourns, let the tears flow. They will always be sacred, the tears of a mother. May God keep count of them; they will be the stars of her crown.

"Un Héros italien de la grande guerre," par Francesco Picco: *Revue politique et littéraire.*

AN ANONYMOUS SOLDIER

The letters of an unnamed soldier to his mother are literature. The young soldier was a painter, but the war made him a poet. It is doubtful if he ever would have painted pictures more beautiful than many in these letters: "Soft weather after rain. Bells in the evening; flowing waters singing under the bridges; trees settling to sleep." He writes to his mother: "There were three of us: we two and the pretty landscape from my window."

This French soldier cannot bring himself to write about the horrors of the war. He prefers to consider "the certainties the tempest has made clear to me." These certainties, from which he never swerves, are "duty and effort." After five days of horror, in which his company was cut to pieces, 1,200 were killed, not a superior officer remained above him, and his captain fell before his eyes just as he was telling him he would report him for citation — the most he has to tell is that he has done his duty.

His whole effort is to raise his soul where events can have no empire over it. "We must feel," he writes to his mother, "that all human uprooting is a little thing, and what is truly ourselves is the life of the soul. . . . Nothing attacks the soul." Although "we lead the life of rabbits on the first day of the season's shooting, notwithstanding that, we can enrich our souls in a magnificent way."

An Englishman, A. Clutton-Brock, says of these letters that before the war — not comprehending so well then — an Anglo-Saxon would have said of them that they are "very French"; that is to say, very unlike what an Englishman (or an American) would write to his mother, or indeed to any one. An Englishman having the same abhorrence of war as this Frenchman, Mr. Clutton-Brock says, would be a conscientious objector. But although he uses the words "torment" and "sacrifice" in connection with himself in the war, he is in it of his own free will — and for all his soul's worth.

One of the first letters says: "Know that it would be shameful to think for one instant of holding back when the race demands the sacrifice." And again: "If you knew the shame I should endure to think that I might have done something more." "O, my beautiful country, the heart of the world," he apostrophizes France in many beautiful passages, and says it needed only "the horror" to make him know "how filial and profound are the ties" which bind him to it.

Only once is he plainly rebellious — and then, oddly enough, he is most human and appealing. "But, oh dearest mother, the war is long, too long for men who had something else to do in the world!" But even then he is not like Jephthah's daughter who asked "for a brief respite to bewail her youth." "No, no," he writes, "I will not mourn over my dead youth." And he recognizes the duty of "accepting the mission in life that presents itself." Only he would have liked to have been one of the torch-bearers, to have carried the flag.

The French soldier has not been heard of since one of the severe battles in the Argonne, in April, 1915. Since he himself is thus one of the missing, it is significant to find him writing to his mother, in one of his many efforts to have them make their grief, and even their love, impersonal, the following: " I hope that when you think of me, you will have in mind all those who have left everything behind; their family, their surroundings, their whole social environment; all those of whom their nearest and dearest think only in the past, saying, ' We had once a brother, who many years ago, withdrew from the world; we know nothing of his fate.' " The words may serve as an epitaph.

(*Letter of Anonymous French Soldier*)

January 23, 1915.

When my trials become less hard, then I begin to think, to dream, and the past that is dear to me seems to have that same remote poetry which in happier days drew my thoughts to distant countries. A familiar street, or certain well-known corners, spring suddenly to my mind — just as in other days islands of dreams and legendary countries used to rise at the call of certain music and verse. But now there is no need of verse or music; the intensity of dear memories is enough.

I have not even any idea of what a new life could be; I only know that we are making life here and now.

For whom and for what age? It hardly matters. What I do know, and what is affirmed in the very depths of my being, is that this harvest of French genius will be safely stored, and that the intellect of our race will not suffer for the deep cuts that have been made in it.

Who will say that the rough peasant, comrade of the fallen thinker, will not be the inheritor of his thoughts. No experience can falsify this magnificent intuition. The peasant's son who has witnessed the death of the young scholar or artist will perhaps take up the interrupted work, be perhaps a link in the chain of evolution which has been for the moment suspended. This is the real sacrifice: to renounce the hope of being the torch-bearer. To a child in a game it is a fine thing to carry the flag; but for a man it is enough to know that the flag will be carried.

And that is what every moment of august Nature brings home to me. Every moment reassures my heart: Nature makes flags of everything. They are more beautiful than those to which our little habits cling.

"Letters of a Soldier." With an Introduction by A Clutton-Brock and a Preface by André Chevrillon. Authorized translation by V. M. Printed by T. and A. Constable at the Edinburgh University Press.

ANTONIO

THERE was a cripple in Rome. His name was Enrico Toti. He was a familiar figure in the Trastevere quarter, where he made little wooden toys and sold them. Insisting upon going to the front, he was at first employed only as a messenger. But it was not long before he was fighting. When he was finally mortally wounded, he cried "Viva l'Italia! Viva Trieste! Viva il Bersagliere!" and he hurled his crutch in the direction of the enemy as he fell.

Many of the Italian letters have this heroic quality, to less impressionable Anglo-Saxon minds it may even seem theatric and familiarly operatic. Most of the letters are frankly nationalistic. Their rallying cry is "Savoia!" "We shout unceasingly 'Savoia! Savoia!'" one of the soldiers writes. The light gleaming on the towers of Trieste is their shining goal. The war for Italy is another war of Italian independence — the fourth. It is the opportunity to destroy once and for all time the reputation of the Italians as a nation of mandolin players, existing for no other purpose than to serenade and amuse the rest of the world. "No! No! We will not be a museum, a hotel, a winter resort, a horizon painted in Prussian blue for international honeymoons!" D'Annunzio said in one of his fiery speeches.

Some of the letters of the Italians are almost child-like in their naiveté and simple faith; others have a wider vision, and all have this note of heroism. A sailor writes to his mother: "But thou must not weep, because one weeps over the tomb of a son who dies, not over that of a soldier who falls in the sacred battle." The "Mama mia" of a letter written by a young Italian prisoner of the dreaded Austrians is as poignant as the similar cry of Turridu in Mascagni's little music drama. It has the essence of poetry.

(*Letter of Antonio, prisoner of the Austrians*)

O Mamma mia, if you could see to what your son is reduced! . . . They have sent me here to dig trenches on the shore of the sea, and when we can do no more they beat us, and the other day two of our number died. O my Mother, I pray you on my knees go every day to the church and pray for your son to the Blessed Virgin of the Rosary, and to our great protector, Saint Anthony, because they alone possess the grace to save thy poor son who is dying of hunger and weakness, for one works fifteen hours a day and they give us to eat three boiled potatoes, and then many beatings.

The other day a fisherman gave me two fishes and I ate them raw, which at one time would have filled me with disgust, but when there is hunger, everything is good.

Yesterday I was thinking so much of my dear

country and of my mother that many tears fell from my eyes, and the sergeant of the guard gave me a kick and wished to throw me into the sea. Oh, Mamma mia, when the weather is fine, I see far, far away across the sea, a strip of land which they have told me is Italy, and I wished to throw myself into the sea and swim to return to my dear country. But the sea is so deep, deep, and I do not know how to swim, and I can do nothing but weep, when I see how many of my companions are dying. . . .

O dear mother, I wish that I could close my eyes for always, so that I could not see any more of this wretchedness, but I think of thee and of my dear country, and of the hearth where we sat to tell stories, and I think of Angiolina whom I love so well, and whom I have promised to marry. And now I pray so much to the Blessed Virgin of the Rosary and to our Lord Jesus, who has had thorns on His head and has suffered so greatly, that He will give me strength to support this anguish. And also, thou, my mother, pray for thy dear son that he may not close his eyes in this inferno, and that he may return home safe and sound. Keep well, my mother, and receive many kisses and embraces from thy unhappy prisoner son. Farewell, farewell — Thy son Antonio.

Taken by permission from "We of Italy," by Klyda Richardson Steege. Published by E. P. Dutton & Company.

ROBERT LE ROUX

HUGUES LE ROUX, one of the editors of the *Matin* in Paris, and French man of letters well known in this country, lost his only son in the early days of the war. Robert Le Roux's first letter is dated August 2, 1914, which shows that he was in at the beginning. His parting words to his father were: "You know that I shall do my duty, and a little more if I have the chance."

He did the little more. He received his death wound at the first contact with the enemy, while leading his men in an heroic charge. On September 26, 1914, M. Le Roux received a letter from his son in hospital which said: "I have been wounded in the arm, but that is nothing. Another bullet passed through the lungs; the spine is bad. This is tiresome, for my legs are paralyzed. But they tell me that, as the wound is a clean one, I shall recover. That is all. I am able to write you owing to the kindness of Mr. N——, one of the officials of the hospital." The signature of the letter was unsteady, and enclosed was a note from "Mr. N——" saying he had written at the boy's dictation, and that he had no chance.

The young sub-lieutenant had kept his diary until a few days before he fell on the field of honor. In his last hours, while the paralysis was creeping towards his heart, he told his father the rest of the story, which M. Le Roux wrote down exactly as he told it, under pretence of sending to his fiancée. Just before he died, the boy raised up in his bed and cried out, almost violently, as his father says, " Come, come! She is bigger now, is she not?" And when his father asked " Who is bigger," he made a supreme effort, and said " France! "

(*Letter of Robert Le Roux*)

You know as well as I do that the instinctive moment at such a time doesn't carry you forward. I thought of you, of Mamma, of Guy, of Marie-Rose, and of Helen. I said to you in my heart: " It is for you! "— and then, my eyes closed, I plunged forward!

The wood was behind us. We were crawling in the open.

You know the maneuver: the moment there is a lull, you bound forward on all fours. I was in the midst of my men. We advanced as though we were swimming.

The horizon was hidden by a hilltop which at about three hundred meters from us rose up against the sky. The Germans, who were entrenched behind the slope, had plenty of time to take good aim at us as though we were so many hares started up. . . .

I did not stop to count those who fell. I cried out: "Closer! Closer!"—and I threw myself ahead of the men to encourage them. Thus bounding on, in a series of leaps, we covered about two hundred meters, and started to crawl up the slope. At each move my section was thinning out, but the men followed me. . . .

One grows accustomed to everything. . . .

Now it seemed as though the bullets were not intended for me. I could see myself at the top of the hill already. . . .

I opened my mouth to call out again: "Onward, my boys!"—when a column of earth and dust passed over us and glued us to the ground. The Boches had brought up their machine guns. In addition, the rain was rattling down. . . .

I threw off the earth that had fallen on me. I seized by his shoulders a soldier lying on my right. I did the same for a man on my left, and the others —they did not move. They stared at me with their poor eyes. I could not tell whether they had been killed or had died of fright.

For a moment I was in despair. This was not what they had pledged me. I stood up in the hailing bullets and shouted with all my strength: "If I am killed, it is your fault!—But as long as you lie there, I shall remain standing!" . . .

They roused themselves; again we moved forward. . . .

I thought to myself: The sergeant won't come back and the major is dying. I must go to them and lose no time about it, otherwise I shall not know whether he wants me to go across the hill.

So I got up, and in order to hasten matters, instead of creeping over the ground, I ran toward my chief. I did not go far. . . .

Taken by permission from "On the Field of Honor," by Hugues Le Roux   Translated by Mrs. John Van Vorst. Published by Houghton Mifflin & Company.

GASTON RIOU

I greet you, sentinel, on the bridge of Europe,
Live bird in your vines, lark in your field.
Cock singing at dawn of the centuries on your farm;
And as a peasant entering the hall
Out of respect for the masters of the house
And that he may not soil the finely waxed floor
Carefully removes his boots and holds them in his hand,
So in your honor, O France, I put aside
The heavy perturbation of my spirit;
The gaze with which I look upon you shall be clear,
My eyes shall look with love, O cherished country!

O ancient wisdom built up century after century;
O courage of the world, heart of the West,
Nation inventive, intelligent, O Living One —
Republic, I hail you by your glorious name.
  — HENRI FRANCK, quoted by Pierre de Lanux.

IN one year, Gaston Riou went on an official mission to Germany. He visited its principal cities and met and talked with its principal scholars and foremost men, including, among many others, a cousin of the former chancellor, Bethmann-Hollweg. The following year Gaston Riou was squatting, as he writes, in the dark corner of a crypt, hungry, thirsty, stupefied. He was a prisoner of war in a Bavarian fortress. He was in Fort Orff eleven months, and had time to think of the many talks of the year before, when the Germans, almost unanimously, had told him that the future was Germany's who would succeed " the aged and dying France."

Gaston Riou, as it happened, was one of the young Frenchmen who thought otherwise, who believed passionately in the France of to-morrow. M. Émile Faguet writes of Riou: " His ardor, his fire, his impetus, the rush of his blood, are all instinct with the passion of patriotism." The year before the war, in 1913, he had written a book called " Aux Écoutes de la France qui vient," in which he said some things that were later to be regarded prophecy: that " a splendid to-morrow worthy of the finest epochs of our history is now germinating in the furrows of the motherland." The book was widely discussed, and Karl Lamprecht, the Pan-German historian, delivered two lectures on it. It is dedicated to the Italian historian, Ferrero.

Gaston Riou was one of the first to go to the war. He took part in the fighting in Lorraine and was mentioned in the dispatches. His entire division was wiped out. He was wounded and taken prisoner in the battle of Dieuze, the little Lorraine town where only the week before a joyous welcome had been given to the French. Pay for a book! " Oh, Monsieur, I could not take money from a French soldier!" Instead, the girl gave him a goblet of Moselle.

In Riou's letters and diary, prison fare is the chief topic. He says: " It seems strange to a man who believed himself to live on ideas to be reduced to become nothing but a stomach." He tells of the "cheese evenings," when the half of a Gruyère cheese was the entire dinner for four hundred and eighty men. But the prisoners are cheerful, and when the Russians arrive, they not only share with them, but scrub them! And the Russians are grateful. The men formed in line to receive their rations. The procession lasted an hour, "as at a great funeral." The "frivolous and impious" Frenchmen, as they hold out their basins, say "The Holy Water," for the soup; and "the handful of earth" for the three ounces of meat.

(Letter of Gaston Riou)

... But imprisonment is above all things hunger, chronic hunger. Those only who have experienced it can understand the effect which chronic hunger speedily exercises even upon an active brain. At first it induces hallucinations. With terrible realism, the sufferer recalls meals eaten before the war, some particular dinner, such and such a picnic. The nerves of taste and smell, exasperated by the scanty regimen, are visited by memories of odors and tastes. The man thinks of nothing but eating. Literally he is nothing but a clamorous stomach. He will lie awake the entire night thinking only of this: "What can I do to-morrow morning to secure a supplementary loaf?

Little Brissot, my friend of the Alpine infantry, when we were walking a few days ago, with our two medical officers, made the unexpected confession:

"Only one thing can give me pleasure now — to get food. Only one man interests me — the man who is capable of getting me food."

This calm declaration from one so highly cultured that he will distract his mind from the cares of important business by reading James and Bergson, from one intimately acquainted with Montaigne and the Lake poets, seemed to us neither paradoxical, nor irrelevant, nor cynical.

... Our rations are dwindling. This morning the quartermaster delivered to the kitchen staff so scanty an allowance of coffee and roasted barley that it hardly seemed to darken the water in our eight cauldrons. On Sunday each man had to be content with 1⅓ oz. of semolina at midday, and with ⅔ oz. of vermicelli in the evening. And what are we to think of this heap of potatoes on the ground at my feet? Is it intended to feed five hundred men or one section? — It is hardly an exaggeration to say we are starving. ...

... Our dietary is still further reduced. To-day we had some horrible little prunes, two years old and hard as wood, in lieu of meat. ...

"The Diary of a French Private," by Gaston Riou. Translated by Eden and Cedar Paul. London: George Allen & Unwin, Ltd.

A GERMAN PRISONER IN FRANCE

THE British Tommies have been accused of making pets of their German prisoners, immediately putting cigarettes into their mouths and buying food and drink for them. A letter written by a young German prisoner to his mother also pays fine tribute to the French care of the German prisoners and wounded. Owing to his great love for the Fatherland, the German prisoner tells his mother that his heart had " wavered and struggled," up to the moment when it " was conquered by this eternal recognition that I owe to the country that has taken in the wounded that their countrymen left on the ground to die like dogs." The letter is quoted by M. Ernest Daudet, and has been stored away in the great and growing " Documents for the History of the War."

(Letter of a German Prisoner in France)

. . . I spent the whole day of Thursday, September 10, and the night of Thursday to Friday, on the battlefield, wrapped in a ragged coat; on Friday afternoon, I was carried to the schoolhouse, converted into a field hospital.

You will permit me, dear parents, not to narrate

to you the manner in which we were abandoned at the time of the retreat of our army. It's a bad business, take my word for it! and far from being to the honor of the German Red Cross which, I think, will not in the future be able to glory in its conduct on the battlefield. Who knows? But you can believe me, the sensations of war are terrible, as for example, to awake one morning and see yourself surrounded by French — and then with nothing more to do! At the military hospital at Bourges, as also at Bar-le-Duc, we were the object of the most assiduous and eager attention. I know your heart, my dear mamma, I know how good you are. Go then also to relieve the misery of the poor French wounded, and do for them as much good as you can. Yes, do it, I beg you, in recognition of what in France they have done for your son . . . it occurs to me that there are some French books at home; give them, I beg you, for me, to the French wounded, who must be mortally dull, a prey to a terrible homesickness as I am.

"L'Âme française et l'âme allemande." Introduction par M. Ernest Daudet. Paris: Attinger Frères.

ARTHUR GEORGE HEATH

ARTHUR GEORGE HEATH was a fellow and tutor at New College, Oxford, when he joined the army in August, 1914. He had a passion for music and a talent for it. He was not a " born soldier." He was one of the many young Oxford and Cambridge men of high promise, sacrificed to the war; whose ideals, as Professor Gilbert Murray says, were gentle, and who were apparently unfitted in mind or body for war, and yet, when the call came, went gayly forth, " as jostling for honor."

When Arthur Heath was killed in France, in October, 1915, many testified to his bravery. It was said his men would have followed him anywhere; perhaps because, as he humorously quotes from a Tommy's letter, he himself was willing to " bear the blunt." His last words were, " Don't trouble about me." A letter written to his mother a few months before he died on his twenty-eighth birthday, is one of the most remarkable and beautiful letters of the war.

(*Letter of Arthur Heath*)

My dear Mother: July 11, 1915.

It is Sunday, and though we shall be working all

the same in a few hours, I feel that I should like to take the opportunity of telling you some things I've wanted to say now for a long time. You remember that I told you when I was going that nothing worried me so much as the thought of the trouble I was causing you by going away, or might cause you if I was killed. Now that death is near I feel the same. I don't think for myself that I've more than the natural instinct of self-preservation, and I certainly do not find the thought of death a great terror that weighs on me. I feel rather that, if I were killed, it would be you and those that love me, that would have the real burden to bear, and I am writing this letter to explain why, after all, I do not think it should be regarded as merely a burden. It would, at least, ease my feelings to try and make the explanation. We make the division between life and death as if it were one of dates — being born at one date and dying some years after. But just as we sleep half our lives, so when we're awake, too, we know that often we're only half alive. Life, in fact, is a quality rather than a quantity, and there are certain moments of real life whose value seems so great that to measure them by the clock, and find them to have lasted so many hours or minutes, must appear trivial and meaningless. Their power, indeed, is such that we cannot properly tell how long they last, for they can color all the rest of our lives, and remain a source of strength and joy that you know not to be exhausted, even though you cannot trace exactly how it works. The first time I ever heard Brahms' Requiem remains with me as an instance of what I mean. Afterwards you do not look back on such events as mere past things whose position in time can be localized; you still feel as living the power that first awoke in them. Now if such moments could be preserved, and the rest strained off, none of us could wish for anything better. . . . And just as these moments of joy or elevation may fill our own lives, so, too, they may be prolonged in the experience of our friends, and, exercising their power in those lives, may know a continual resurrection. You won't mind a personal illustration. I know that one of the ways I live in the truest sense is in the enjoyment of music. Now just as the first hearing of the Requiem was for me more than an event which passed away, so I would like to hope that my love of music might be for those who love and survive me more than a memory of something past, a power rather that can enhance for them the beauty of music itself. Or, again, we love the South Down country. Now I would hate to think that, if I died, the "associations" would make these hills "too painful" for you, as people sometimes say. I would like to think the opposite, that the joy I had in the Downs might not merely be remembered by you as a fact in the past, but rather be, as it were, transfused into you and give a new quality of happiness to your holidays there. . . . Will you at least try, if I am killed, not to let the things I have loved, cause you pain, but rather to get increased enjoyment from the Sussex Downs or from Janie singing folk songs, because I have found such joy in them, and in that way the joy I have found can continue to live.

And again, do not have all this solemn funeral music, Dead Marches, and so on, played over me as if to proclaim that all has now come to an end, and nothing better remains to those who loved one than a dignified sorrow. I would rather have the Dutch Easter Carol, where the music gives you the idea of life and joy springing up continually.

And if what I have written seems unreal and fantastic to you, at least there's one thing with which you'll agree. The will to serve now is in both of us, and you approve of what I'm doing. Now that is just one of the true and vital things that must not be, and is not exhausted by the moment at which it is felt or expressed. My resolution can live on in yours, even if I am taken, and, in your refusal to regret what we know to have been a right decision, it can prove itself undefeated by death.

Please forgive me if I have worried you by all this talk. If we loved one another less I could not have written this, and, just because we love one

another, I cannot bear to think that, if I died, I should only give you trouble and sorrow. . . . .
All my love to you,
ARTHUR.

Taken by permission from "Letters of Arthur George Heath" With memoir by Gilbert Murray. Published by Longmans, Green & Company.

OBSERVER B—— de P——

M. Victor Giraud, who has collected a good many French war letters, says of a letter written by a young aviator that nothing " more young, more fresh, more noble, and more pure " has come to his notice; and he suggests that we do not often think enough of the parents and grandparents of these heroes; of the long line of " traditions, obscure devotions, secret virtues," of which they are the happy outcome and the witness. The boy's name is not given, although in his letter he says the great general who decorated him said the name was not unknown to him, and we learn that his father was a brave man before him. Such a letter, as M. Giraud says, does as much honor to the family that received it as to the son who wrote it:

(Letter of Observer B—— de P——)

All my happiness is increased by the honor I am going to do to my old warrior father by this cross that is going to shine on my breast. I have been officially cited for the legion of honor. I shall have it in a few days. I am very proud. I had the choice between promotion and the cross. So much the worse for the stripes! Papa often said to me: " It is a piece of foolishness; but, my faith, it is chic, it tempts and delights me; the stripes are money, this cross is glory."

I am still a little under the shock of the emotion, and I hardly know how to tell it all to you. I have not slept this night. I kept seeing the poor enemy awaited on the other side by their own, and I knew the anxiety that crushes you when one of our "birds" is across the enemy's lines and is a long time coming back. I thought of their mothers, of their sisters, of their wives perhaps. . . .

There was a pilot, a lieutenant; and the observer, a captain. We met about 2,700 meters up. I had thrown overboard glasses, gloves, and the whole business! I was able to fire four shots, and three hit. One killed dead the captain-observer, straight in the heart; another broke one of the pilot's arms, at the same time piercing his reservoir; the third passed through his neck. They went down like a water-spout; but the pilot, very skillful, was able to make a landing with one arm, and the machine was uninjured. We swooped down after them like a vulture after its prey; it was magnificent. Never, never can you imagine what it was.

On the ground, I leaped out of my machine. The observer, dead at his post, was lifeless. The pilot salutes and surrenders. My faith! You will laugh, but I fell upon that young fellow, and shook his hand with all my strength. He understood, and I saw in his eyes that he knew what was passing in my heart.

In the evening, the commanding general summoned to headquarters the pilot (Gilbert) and myself, and congratulated us warmly; it was de Castelnau. Our name was not unknown to him, he told me. He was very nice, and I assure you it is an interview not soon to be forgotten. I would like it if the cross I am going to wear could be one of those that Papa wore for so long; can you not find me one of those croix de chevalier?

I haven't the time to write more. I am a little unnerved, but very well, and contented, and happy in your happiness. May dear Papa also be happy! I thought of him also up there, at the great moment of the attack. I had good chances not to return. Sweet and fleeting images, your features, and your names, were in my heart during my last prayer up there, up there! It was solemn and sweet, and as always I have been protected, blessed. Thanks, dear God! Thanks for your tenderness, your prayers, your love which make me so strong, so brave.

"Lettres du Front," par Victor Giraud, *Revue des Deux Mondes.*

"GOD PUNISH ENGLAND!"

IN a new volume of the Oxford Dictionary, Vol. IX., the word "Strafe" appears for the first time:

"Strafe (straf), v. slang. [From the Ger. phrase Gott strafe England, 'God Punish England,' a common salutation in Germany in 1914 and the following years.] Used (originally by British soldiers in the war against Germany) in various senses suggested by its origin: To punish; to do damage to; to attack fiercely; to heap imprecations on. . . ."

Among the citations given is one from the *London Times Literary Supplement:* "The Germans are called the Gott-strafers, and strafe is becoming a comic English word"; and another from the *London Daily Mail:* "The word strafe is now almost universally used. Not only is an effective bombardment of the enemy's lines or a successful trench raid described by Tommy as 'strafing the Fritzes,' but there are occasions when certain 'brass hats' are strafed by imprecation. And quite recently the present writer heard a working-class woman shout to one of her offspring, 'Wait till I git 'old of yer, I'll strarfe yer, I will!'"

London Punch printed a picture showing a German family going through its "morning hate" ceremonies. It all sounds like something out of a comic weekly, but in its issue of December 5, 1914, the *Norddeutsche Allgemeine Zeitung* printed the following letter from the front written by a lieutenant of the landwehr to the *Hanover Advertiser:*

(Letter of " God Punish England!")

As a good Hanoverian I send you from French soil the heartiest, true-German greeting, and beg you to grant a modest corner to the following lines:

"GOD PUNISH ENGLAND!" "MAY HE PUNISH HER!"

That is the new greeting of our troops. Suggested by some one or other, it is spreading. He who hears it for the first time is surprised, understands, and it goes further on its round. Everywhere here, when an officer or private enters a room, he does not say " Good day," or even " Adieu" when he goes out, but " God punish England!" and the answer, " May He punish her!" Oh, it is pleasant to German ears, and the customary greeting has seldom been so much reflected upon, as now. " May He punish her!" Yes, indeed, that is what we want, and that is why we Germans have come away, and left our home and our families, to punish all who have robbed us of peace.

And you dear ones at home, you men who remain behind, keep it before your eyes. Our motto is, like yours, " God punish England!" And when you are sitting at your usual table in the restaurant, think of it. Don't say, "Prosit," when you drink; no, do like us, say, "God punish England!" and answer, "May He punish her!"

It refreshes the heart, when the company-leader greets his company in the morning. Instead of wishing a good morning, for every morning close to the enemy is to us a good-morning; we do not need to wish one another that. But an iron voice rings across the market-place of V.: "Attention! God punish England!" and from three hundred throats there meets us the cry: "May He punish her!"

Perhaps the greeting will also take up its abode in our dear Hanover for the period of the campaign, and perhaps other newspapers and other German districts will take up the suggestion. And with this good-by. "May He punish her!"

— Printed in the *Norddeutsche Allgemeine Zeitung,* Dec. 5, 1914.

Taken by permission from "A Month's German Newspapers," selected and translated by Adam L. Gowans. Published by Frederick A. Stokes Company.

PIERRE-MAURICE MASSON

THE tragic sense of loss is in no case felt more than in the story of Pierre-Maurice Masson, professor of French literature at the University of Fribourg, and the author of many noteworthy biographical studies. In the summer of 1916, Lieutenant Masson was expecting a permit to return to the "trenches of the Sorbonne," as he phrased it, to receive his doctor's degree. He had corrected and read the proof of his master work on Rousseau at the front, and now, as he wrote to his friends, "The monster is ready!"

But he did not get his permit. The activity of the Crown Prince at Verdun caused all permits to be recalled. "Man proposes," he writes, "and the Boches dispose." Inclined to fret a little at first, he nevertheless says that his bad luck is a mere bagatelle compared with "the future of the world"; and when he gets the command of his company, he is wholly content and writes that he has become resigned, and no longer thinks of anything but the war. "I send to the devil the Sorbonne and likewise the permits, and I only desire to attend strictly to my business. It is a hard and beautiful business, and I would not give my place commanding the company for all the sinecures back there."

Pierre-Maurice Masson was a son of Lorraine, having been born at Metz in 1879. He was one of the Alsace-Lorraine "protesters." He was for "la revanche," but for the "revenge of justice," as he said. In 1911, he wrote that the time for all silence and restraint was past, and that France should not be afraid to say, "We do not accept the brigandage and we demand the return of our stolen property." Justice is the word most frequently found in his letters. The war must not be terminated until justice is done. "We have suffered too much in the name of justice," he writes to his wife, "to accept a peace without it." Of one of his friends killed in the war he writes that he has "waked in that eternal serenity that awaits the defenders of justice." He tells his wife that whatever happens they must have courage and "hold to the end."

It was his strong sense of justice, no doubt, that explains Lieutenant Masson's unusually (even for the French) sympathetic relations with the men he commanded. "This equality in the anonymous peril," he writes, "has something fraternal about it that is very salutary." Just because he will leave a few "old books" behind, he does not believe makes his life worth any more than that of the men whose uncomplaining heroism he is never tired of praising. Some of them know that their villages have been burned, their homes pillaged, that their wives and children have fled — they know not where — and yet they refuse to think of anything but of "la patrie," and its welfare. Every time he talks with the soldiers — and there is time, he says, to talk on the long night marches — he feels himself inferior. And this is the reason, as he writes to his wife, why he tries to do little things for them, show interest in their lives and families and worries, "and," he adds almost naively, "they feel, I think, that this interest is sincere."

M. Victor Giraud, whom Professor Masson succeeded at Fribourg, says that his letters are among the most beautiful of the war letters, and that one of them at least is destined to become classic: the description he wrote to his wife of the trenches at Fleury, where he later lost his life.

(Letter of Pierre-Maurice Masson)

Through shining acres of the musket spears—
Where flame and wither with swift intercease
Flowers of red sleep that not the cornfield bears—
— FRANCIS THOMPSON.

June 19, 1915.

I find your letter on returning from our visit to the Fleury trenches. We left in an automobile at two o'clock this morning, and were for three and a half hours in the trenches that face Fort-Marre. It is one of the most active sectors in all this part, one of those where the bombardment is continuous; it is precisely for that reason that we made our visit at dawn, because this is the time when both sides, by mutual agreement, each worn out by the hard night, drops guns, mortars and grenades, and goes to sleep. And, in fact, it was very quiet all the time we were there, but the stretcher-bearers who were coming down, just as we arrived, testified to the activity of the night. I see again, especially, in one of the narrow trenches, carried by two men in a sail cloth, like some poor dead game, a sort of human rag, that a shell has pulverized. But what is one dead in this vast cemetery! The first line trench that has been captured from the Germans, and that has seen some furious, hand-to-hand fighting, several times changing hands, is only an ancient charnel house, where the walls, the parapets, the loop-holes are builded of human dough. One still sees, here and there, a foot sticking out, a back humped into a piece of buttress. Little by little, all the wretchedness has been concealed by being clothed with sand bags, but it is only a poor screen. The frightful acrid odor that chokes you, the incessant buzzing of great green flies that swarm over the débris, are enough to remind you where you are. And to tell that men live here, in this cadaverous earth, in this tragic plague spot, which the sun fecundates and spreads! Along the narrow trench one sees men pass with the little copper sprayers that the vine dressers use when they go to spray the vines; they sprinkle with chloride of lime and disinfectants the vines of the dead. And, moreover, the genuine vine of Toul still grows here. In this earth enriched by blood and baked by the sun, everything has rank growth. Between the parapets, among the old bags, the abandoned equipment, in the rottenness and the rubbish, in the midst of the chaos dug by the shells, one sees the roots of vines, or rather new shoots of a veritable green growth. Further there are a lot of potato sprouts, and above all fields of wild poppies, of a glorious red, blazing, that seem the blooming of all the blood that has watered this ground. How a human life seems a small thing, an insignificant thing, in this jumble of corpses, of spring-time renewal, and careless happy existence! For all along this bloody labyrinth, young poilus, who do not say all that they feel, and who perhaps no longer feel, sleep peacefully, laugh, or play "manille," while waiting for the shell that is going to kill them.

"Lettres de Guerre." Pierre-Maurice Masson. Préface de Victor Giraud. Notice biographique par Jacques Zeiller. Paris: Librairie Hachette.

CONINGSBY DAWSON

"AND was I really the budding novelist in New York?" Coningsby Dawson writes in one of his letters. But he was more than the "budding novelist." The first novel he wrote, "The Garden Without Walls," had an immediate and enviable success. In interrupting his career to enter the war, he probably gave up more than most. Yet, from the mud banks of the Somme, he exclaims, apparently with innermost conviction: "The insufficiency of merely setting nobilities down on paper!" and in another letter, with equal conviction: "O, if I get back, how differently I shall write!"

Coningsby Dawson was graduated from Oxford with honors in 1905, and in the same year came to the United States with the intention of studying for the ministry. But after a year at a Theological Seminary, he decided upon a literary career, which he was pursuing with great earnestness and good promise, when the war came. In the introduction to his book "Carry On," his father writes: "From the very first he saw clearly where his duty lay." He enlisted with the Canadian Field Artillery.

(*Letter of Coningsby Dawson*)

September 15th, 1916.

Dear Father:

It's a fortnight to-day since I left England, and

already I've seen action. Things move more quickly in this game — one which brings out both the best and the worst qualities in a man. If unconscious heroism is the virtue most to be desired, and heroism spiced with a strong sense of humor at that, then pretty well every man I have met out here has the amazing guts to wear his crown of thorns as though it were a cap-and-bells. To do that for the sake of corporate stout-heartedness is, I think, the acme of what Aristotle meant by virtue. A strong man, or a good man or a brainless man, can walk to meet pain with a smile on his mouth because he knows that he is strong enough to bear it, or worthy enough to defy it, or because he is such a fool that he has no imagination. But these chaps are neither particularly strong, good, or brainless; they're more like children, utterly casual with regard to trouble, and quite aware that it is useless to struggle against their elders. So they have the merriest of times while they can, and when the governess, Death, summons them to bed, they obey her with unsurprised quietness. It sends the mercury of one's optimism rising to see the way they do it. I search my mind to find the bigness of motive which supports them, but it forever evades me. These lads are not the kind who philosophize about life; they're the sort, many of them, who would ordinarily wear corduroys and smoke a cutty pipe. I suppose the Christian martyrs would have done the same had corduroys been the fashion in that day, and if a Roman Raleigh had discovered tobacco. . . .

Ever yours, with love,
Con.

Taken by permission from "Carry On," by Coningsby Dawson. Published by John Lane Company.

A SAINT-CYRIEN

THE famous vow of the Saint-Cyriens — the young French officers corresponding to American West-Pointers — is that they will go into battle wearing their white gloves and their red and white plumes in their caps. And as they go gallantly forth to battle, in all their bravery, so they ask the people at home to put on their gala attire to meet them on their return.

It was a Saint-Cyrien who wrote: "When the troops come home victorious through the Arc de Triomphe, put on your finest apparel and be there." And another wrote: "We shall perhaps not be there, but others will be there for us. Do not weep, do not wear mourning, for we shall have died with a smile on our lips and a superhuman joy in our heart. Vive la France! Vive la France!"

How well the injunction has been obeyed is illustrated in the story that has been told many times of the young French wife, searching the faces of the marching soldiers for her husband; and who, when one stepped out of the ranks to tell her that her husband had been killed the day before, raised her child high in her arms and cried: " Vive la France!"

In the following letter written by a Saint-Cyrien, by name Gaston Voizard, M. Barrès, who quotes it, says he seems almost to apologize for outliving some of his brother officers by a few months. The letter is written on Christmas night, 1914. His turn did not come until the following April. The letter is one of the few addressed to a "demoiselle"; most of the letters, of the Frenchmen especially, are written to mothers:

(*Letter of a Saint-Cyrien*)

December 25, 1918.

It is midnight, Mademoiselle and good friend, and in order to write to you I have just removed my white gloves. (This is not a bid for admiration. The act has nothing of the heroic about it; my last colored pair adorn the hands of a poor foot-soldier [piou-piou] who was cold.)

I am unable to find words to express the pleasure and emotion caused me by your letter which arrived in the evening following a terrific bombardment of the poor little village we are holding. The letter was accepted among us as a balm for all possible racking of nerves and other curses. That letter, which was read in the evening to the officers of my battalion,— I ask pardon for any offense to your modesty,— comforted the most cast-down after the hard day and gave proof to all that the heart of the young girls of France is nothing short of magnificent in its beneficence.

It is, as I have said, midnight. To the honor and good fortunes which have come to me of commanding my company during the last week (our captain having been wounded) I owe the pleasure of writing you at this hour from the trenches, where by prodigies of cunning, I have succeeded in lighting a candle without attracting the attention of the gentlemen facing us, who are, by the way, not more than a hundred meters distant.

My men, under their breath, have struck up the traditional Christmas hymn, " He is born, the Child Divine." The sky glitters with stars. One feels like making merry over all this, and, behold, one is on the brink of tears. I think of Christmases of other years spent with my family; I think of the tremendous effort still to be made, of the small chance I have for coming out of this alive; I think, in short, that perhaps this minute I am living my last Christmas.

" Regret," do you say? . . . No, not even sadness. Only a tinge of gloom at not being among those I love.

All the sorrow of my thoughts is given to those best of friends fallen on the field of honor, whose loyal affection has made them almost my brothers; — Allard, Fayolle, so many dear friends whom I shall never see again! When on the evening of July 31, in my capacity of " Père Système " of the promotion, I had pronounced amid a holy hush the famous vow to make ourselves conspicuous by facing death wearing white gloves, our good-hearted

Fayolle, who was, I may say, the most of an enthusiast of all the friends I have ever known, said to me with a grin: "What a stunning impression we shall make upon the Boches! They will be so astounded that they will forget to fire." But, alas, poor Fayolle has paid dearly his debt to his country, for the title of Saint-Cyrien! And they are all falling around me, seeming to ask when the time of their "Père Système" is to come, so that "Montmirail"[1] on entering Heaven may receive God's blessing with full ranks.

But a truce to useless repinings! Let us give thought only to our dear France, our indispensable, imperishable, ever-living country! And, by this beauteous Christmas night, let us put our faith more firmly than ever in victory.

I must ask you, Mademoiselle and good friend, to excuse this awful scrawl. Will you allow me to hope for a reply in the near future, and will you permit this young French officer very respectfully to kiss the hand of a great-souled and generous-hearted maiden of France?

Taken by permission from "The Undying Spirit of France," by Maurice Barrès. Translated by Margaret W. B. Corwin. With a Foreword by Theodore Stanton. Published by the Yale University Press.

[1] Name of the class at Saint Cyr.

ROBERT ERNEST VERNÈDE

Little you'd care what I laid at your feet,
  Ribbon or crest or shawl —
What if I bring you nothing, sweet,
  Nor maybe come home at all?
Ah, but you'll know, Brave Heart, you'll know
  Two things I'll have kept to send:
My honor, for which you bade me go,
  And my love — my love to the end.
                                R. E. VERNÈDE.

SOME one has said that middle age, always a blunder, has become since the war a sort of crime. But for Robert Ernest Vernède, his nearly forty years were neither. Although four years over age, he enlisted early in the war as a private. Edmund Gosse, who has written in praise of "the generous gesture," with which the youth of the world "greeted the sacrifice of their hopes and ours," says some praise should be reserved for those who having been brought face to face with the illusions of youth, had "got into the habit of not being soldiers."

Robert Ernest Vernède's habits were the furthest from a soldier's. When the war came, he was married and deep in a Hertfortshire garden. He was an Oxford man, a novelist and a poet. He was born in London in 1875, but was of French extraction. Robert Louis Stevenson, in his "Travels With a Donkey," mentions the ancestral castle of the

Vernèdes. He not only went to the war voluntarily, but having returned home wounded once, he went again, and this time he did not return. He was killed leading an attack on Havrincourt Wood, April 9, 1916. "It was thus," his friend Chesterton writes, "that he passed from the English country life he loved so much, with its gardening and dreaming, to an ambush and a German gun."

His letters were written to his wife. They are filled with his contentment with what he is doing, and with his admiration for the fighting men. He thinks the men are " wonderful and awfully good to one another." Even the cook exposes himself to danger to assist the stretcher-bearers — " which I'm afraid will render me weak-minded towards his cookery in the future." He writes: " The only cheerful thing is the sun, when it appears, and the men whose cheeriness is unending." Nor is it " the sort of heedless gayety I used to suspect them of, but a gallant effort to make the best of things, and not let their morale fall below an ideal." He himself is always " in the pink," as he is fond of saying, and he quotes from a Tommy's letter: " Dear Mum and Dad, and dear loving sisters Rosie, Letty, and our Gladys. I hope you keeps the home fires burning. Not arf. The boys are in the pink. Not arf."

More than to most, the issues of the war were simple, direct and clear to this Englishman: a case of right and wrong, darkness and light, democratic civilization and dynastic and military rule. Of one of his poems, " Before the Assault," written at the front, and acknowledged to be one of the finest of the war poems, Chesterton says: "No printed controversy or political eloquence could put more logically, let alone more poetically, the higher pacifism which is resolute to dry up at the fountain head the bitter waters of the dynastic wars than these four lines:

> Then to our children there shall be no handing
>   Of fates so vain — of passions so abhorr'd —
> But Peace — the Peace which passeth understanding —
>   Not in our time — but in their time, O Lord.

In one of the letters, he refers to this poem:

(Letter of Robert Ernest Vernède)

I rather foresee a time (after Peace) when people will be sick of the name of War — won't hear a word of it or anything connected with it. There seem to be such people now, and I see numbers of silly books and papers advertised as having nothing to do with the war. It's natural, perhaps, that soldiers should want a diversion and even civilians; but I rather hope that people won't altogether forget it in our generation. That's what I wanted to say in the verses I began about —

> Not in our time, O Lord, we now beseech Thee
> To grant us peace — the sword has bit too deep —

but never got on with. What I mean is that for us there can be no real forgetting. We have seen too much of it, known too many people's sorrow, felt it too much to return to an existence in which it has no part. Not that one wants to be morbid about it later; but still less does one want to be as superficial as before. The sword has bit too deep.

"Letters to His Wife," by R. E. Vernède. London: W. Collins & Co.

ANDRÉ CORNET-AUQUIER

ANDRÉ CORNET-AUQUIER was a professor before the war, although before he died he had determined to remain in the army where he thought his country's need was greater. His letters were written from the Alsatian front to his parents. Like so many of these soldiers' letters, especially the French, they are remarkable not only for their spirit but their literary excellence.

Also like so many of the French soldiers, and contrary to popular belief, this young French captain is deeply religious. His faith is unwavering, and he says with him prayer is a "constant state." But if any one thinks his piety interferes with his gayety, he is mistaken. "How I make them laugh," he writes in one letter. He quotes the rules and regulations for the Grand Hotel of the Trenches, how they must not leave the gas burning, nor carry off the sandbags, nor lean out of the windows, nor, especially, have anything to do with the rival concern over the way. He is very sure that the neighbors over the way "are not as gay as we."

The French captain is constantly imploring his parents to be brave, and not let their affection for him be a source of weakness to him, but, on the contrary, an armor. He asks his mother particularly to be "the most French" of all admirable French mothers, and say to herself that "no life whatsoever, not even that of thine own son, is anything in comparison with the salvation of the country."

Captain Cornet-Auquier's last letter, dated February 29, 1916, closes with the words, "I am going to bed without even eating, so weary am I." He was mortally wounded on March 1, and died the next day. He received the war cross and the cross of the Legion of Honor, although he says with all the business in hand, there is not much time to think of honors and advancements. He was twenty-eight.

Perhaps because of the numerous "English uncles," whom he mentions, his idea of what the Allies are fighting for most nearly coincides with that most often expressed by an Englishman or an American — that the war is against war.

(Letter of André Cornet-Auquier)

How I would like to feel that you are ready, even before it comes, to make if necessary the sacrifice of my life. How I would like to be able to say to myself: "At least they are ready, and if my death would be painful to them, they are resigned to it, resigned in advance." I also have moments of impatience, especially when I feel myself so full of youth and strength, when I reflect on all that I have abandoned, of work, hopes, all that future which was smiling on me,— at such moments I wish it were all ended. But this morning I began reflecting on what is the life of an individual in comparison with the general peace of all the nations of Europe,—nothing. . . .

. . . My hour has perhaps not yet sounded. It will probably come. I no longer pray for myself, but for the others, for you all, and for thee, mother, especially; and how ardent, fervent, passionate is that prayer. I ask God to make you all calm and brave whatever happens. I would be a hundredfold stronger if I knew that you were joyously ready. And especially do not look upon me as a hero or a wonder. No. What have I done that is extraordinary? Nothing. I have tried to do my duty like everybody else. That's all. . . . What are our lives worth when we think of the years of happiness and peace of those who will follow us and those who may survive us. We labor for to-morrow, in order that there may be no more wars, no more spilling of blood, no more killing, no more wounded, no more mutilated victims; we labor, we whom our mothers will so weep for, in order that other mamas may never know these bitter tears. In truth, when one thinks of the centuries that this peace will last, one is ashamed of the rebellious movements which the flesh is guilty of at certain moments at the thought of death. . . .

Taken by permission from "A Soldier Unafraid," by Captain André Cornet-Auquier. Translated with an introduction by Theodore Stanton. Published by Little, Brown and Company.

MARCEL ÉTÉVÉ

MARCEL ÉTÉVÉ was a student at the Ecole Normale in Paris. He was an accomplished musician, and had already had some success as a composer. He was twenty-four years old. He was put at the head of his column because of his great height. The part of the trench he occupied, he writes jestingly to a friend, he has had dug deeper, because his head stuck out, and he is too lazy to stoop, and, moreover, he has a right to be comfortable!

"What a bizarre and joyous war, when you think of it from one point of view, and not from another!" We amuse ourselves like "little fools," he says, and "the joys of trench life have hardly been exaggerated." To be sure, he regrets his music, in the midst of the caroming of the cannon and the snoring of the men. But he hopes that what he loses in study he may gain in spontaneity of impressions, if he is ever permitted to "replunge into civilized harmonies"— which is his heart's desire. In the meantime, he reads, everything apparently, including "my dear Kipling."

Lieutenant Étévé was very popular with his men. It is said he never asked them to do anything he did not do himself "at least once." He writes to his mother that the main thing is that they be willing, not afraid, and "love me a little."

Étévé was killed in the Picardy attack in July, 1916. His company had taken almost immediately the enemy's trench, but soon after was cut off from all communication with the rear. For an hour it defended itself with grenades. Already wounded in the shoulder, Lieutenant Étévé was in a good deal of pain, but he kept his command. Second-lieutenant M—— came up to him and said: " My old fellow, if in five minutes we don't get reinforcements, we are dead. We are not going to get them. Adieu." Étévé replied: " I know it, but let us not say anything about it, in order not to discourage the men. Adieu." A few minutes later he received a bullet in the head. His name was given to the trench when it was finally definitely held, and the standard of the company — when it also " died " and was disbanded — to which her son gave its first " ray of glory " was sent to the mother for the school which she directs.

Most of Lieutenant Étévé's letters are written to his mother. They are love letters, like so many of the letters to mothers. " I am decorated," he writes to her; " on my heart are the golden fringes of the flag; in my cartridge box are three little violets filched from your bouquet." He says he can die because " thanks to you, I have already had a life longer and fuller than the majority of men." He says he loves her with all his soul, " which you have fashioned." His last words to her are, " Let us hope, and love each other, hard, hard. . . ."

He had been fortunate in falling in with a group of officers who are so kind, as he tells his mother, and agreeable, and also intellectual. "Not one of them," he says, " is ' militaire ' to excess, and in the worst sense of the word." It was about militarism and frightfulness and " war on war " that he wrote to his friend:

(Letter of Marcel Étévé)

You speak of the " war on war," and you seem to think I do not agree with you. What kind of a brute do you think I am? Is it my little speeches in favor of the poor " meletaires " that warrant you in doing me such an injustice? Could you think that the soldiers I was defending were different from you and me, submitting to the war as the worst of catastrophes; and that I was one of those who see in it the normal employment of their faculties?

However, if it is necessary to make a full confession, perhaps I have something to do with your misunderstanding. For some time, in fact, I tried, half seriously, to acquire, to a certain degree, a mind " for military purposes." But it was not serious, and I never had great confidence in the business. I have, emphatically, not the required " hate."

And I have resolved not to bother any more about it, knowing that I do not need the stimulus. To begin at the bottom, I shall have, in fact, every time that it shall be necessary to strike hard and cruelly, the blind rage of combat, and it is much. In climbing a little higher up the ladder of motives, I shall have also the necessary self-esteem and proper bearing; and that is something to go on. Finally, even from a still more intellectual point of view, I shall have the conscience to perform a necessary duty, and to take part, from this moment, in the " war on war." And let it go at that. . . .

"Lieutenant Marcel Étévé: Lettres d'un Combattant."
Préface de M. Paul Dupuy. Paris: Librairie Hachette.

THE SOLDIER PRIEST

A WORLD war, more than American politics, makes strange bedfellows. A French soldier priest describes the following incident of the retreat from Charleroi: "One evening four of us, a protestant preacher, a rabbi, an officer who called himself a free thinker, and I, had the good luck to find a bed, without any bedding, of course, and a mattress. Quick, quick, let us draw lots: the preacher sleeps with the rabbi (the Old with the New Testament), and Dogma, which I represent, lies down by the side of free thinking. In less than two minutes, there is a wonderful concert, the like of which no great religious congress could produce."

Another story is also told of the dying Catholic soldier who asked the Jewish stretcher-bearer for a crucifix; and the Jew brought a crucifix, and a few moments afterwards was himself hit by a shell, and died in the arms of a Catholic priest. The democratization and fraternization going on in the armies, is thus likewise producing a greater tolerance and sympathy in those of opposing religious beliefs.

In fact, what with the fighting priest, and the chaplain ("Not 'arf," as the British Tommy says, meaning the highest praise), and the Y. M. C. A. young man, and a Cardinal Mercier — one of the great heroes of the great war — all religion is giving a pretty good account of itself in the war, and deserves to be decorated with a special cross — which the Allied armies would hardly use as a movable target to direct their firing, as the Germans used a cross in Flanders.

There are those who believe that anti-clericalism in France especially will be less popular after the war, owing to the heroism and self-sacrificing spirit shown by the fighting priests, who cheerfully acquiesced in the law that made them soldiers, and whose rallying cry as they march to battle is: " Vivent les curés sac au dos!"

Everybody mourns according to his own needs and desires. Brand Whitlock, American minister to former Belgium, tells that the scholarly old priest who described to him the destruction of Ypres, never wavered while he told of his brothers and friends shot down before his eyes; but when he reached the fate of the library, that priceless collection of books, he could not even say the word, but stammered " biblio . . . bib . . ." and bowed his head upon his arms and wept.

A young French priest, Abbé Philippe P——, in writing about Ypres, indulges in a little irony at the expense of "kultur," so long as he is telling about the destruction of the Halles and other buildings. But when he comes to the church —"la maison de Dieu"— this is what touches him most nearly, and it is here that the young priest weeps, and he writes that there must be no weakening until the hour for justice comes, and there is a " healing victory."

(*Letter of a Soldier Priest*)

Ypres! One should pray in this town, as in a temple; it is a shrine, a relic. . . . All is sacred.

Literally, there is not a building that has not been shelled, pierced with bullets, riddled, disemboweled: doorless, windowless, roofless. Ruins of walls; piles of stones; here a broken column lying on the ground, there a portico; everywhere the stigmata of the shells.

They have destroyed for the sake of destroying. There is no excuse for such devastation. Churches, halls, stalls, little homes of small merchants, workshops — why this frightfulness against all these? There is no strategic reason that will hold. Why this rage against a Belgian town, the city of a people drawn into the war in spite of themselves, from whom one only pretended to ask a passage through, and whom one is able to reproach only for being loyal even to sacrifice? It is rage, it is hate, it is madness. It is satanic.

One repeats a thousand times the name of Pompeii in connection with Ypres. It comes spontaneously to the lips. But at Pompeii more things must have been respected. At Pompeii pretty statuettes were found uninjured; you will find none at Ypres. And also, in the case of Pompeii, it was a natural force; it was the volcano; it was the earth giving birth to something; there was still on the horizon a beauty which Pliny could contemplate; it was hot ashes, spouting from the entrails of the earth, and falling like a veil on the city.

At Ypres, it is the work of man against man, human brutality against justice and against beauty; heavy shells of Teuton metal, each seeking out its building, guided by a human will, the work of science in revolt against humanity and against art. No excuse. Nothing but horror. There is only one word that explains it all: sin. The word haunts me like an obsession. . . .

There are great holes everywhere, down low, up high; low in the streets, high in the walls. In what once were houses, are the remains of what once was life: a table, a counter with bottles, shelves of a grocery store, workshops, the thousand little everyday things, curtains, débris of bedding, lace, a piano.

And I reflect: Here was a home, a shelter of love and of hope; there were old people who watched the young growing up while saying: "They will take our place, they will have more comfort, more happiness than we have had." Where are they all now, the big and the little? Just now a man said to me: "I have obtained permission to reënter this house which is mine; my son has been killed, and is lying out there." And his young daughter added, while picking a rose for us: "You see, one cannot be separated from what one has planted." From what one has planted! All the hopes, affections, centered in these homes, now uprooted! All is a desert, all. . . .

Some one near to me asks: "What will one do with these ruins after the war?" And I answered, as if mechanically: "A museum. And one will put over the entrance: Kultur!" It is the inevitable thought of every one in the presence of this devastation. . . .

If there is any irony in me, it lasts only a moment. It is frozen upon my visit to the churches. I have tears in my eyes. It is as if a mailed fist clutched my heart; I can hardly breathe; I grow pale; I am sick physically; I am sick to my soul. I wish I had not entered. I wish I had not seen. . . .

It is necessary to push open what is left of the tottering doors, or mount the piles of stone and go through the breaches in the walls. No longer any altar, a little heap of stones or marble; broken columns lying on the ground; all the stones of a pillar disjointed and thrown down one on top of the other, like a heap of great copper sous spilled out; the stained glass, powder; the lead melted; the railings of the pulpit edentate; the pipes of the organ twisted, and its case suspended in the air; almost all the statues thrown down as if in profanation; here an arm, there a leg, here a torso, there a head.

And such queer freaks of the wreckage; this saint with a crutch, thrown down, as an infirm old man whom the mischievous hand of a child had pushed over; in the arms of the Virgin, an Infant Jesus with the head broken in two, and the fingers of one of the hands broken off while the other still holds the world; it smiles, such a sad little smile! A Virgin has a bullet in her temple; a Saint Roque has an authentic wound, while his dog has a broken foot. There is a new and surprising detail in every statue. . . . The pictures are full of holes; and here is a beautiful tryptych, painted on wood, that holds out its sagging doors like broken wings. . . .

God is then the first victim . . . and it is necessary to live until the hour comes for justice, for a healing victory.

"Lettres de Prêtres aux Armées. Recuillées par Victor Bucaille. Paris: Librairie Payot et Cie.

ROBERT HERTZ

THOSE could hardly have remembered Masada, who thought that the Jews of the Allied nations would not rally with enthusiasm to fight against an enemy threatening to introduce once more race rule in the world. It was after Jerusalem had fallen, nearly two thousand years ago, and Masada was still resisting, that the brave Eleazar summoned the people to the public square and said: "Let us die unenslaved." It was voted that every man should be the executioner of his own family, and every man was; and in turn they killed one another, drawing lots, until at last only one man was left to fall upon his own sword. When the Romans advanced into the city, they found two women and five children, who had concealed themselves in a cave.

One of the most moving letters of the war is written by Robert Hertz, socialist and son of a German Jew, living in and passionately loving France and her free institutions. He fights, as he writes to his wife, that their son may hold his head high, and walk erect, with a firm tread, an equal among free men, because he will be able to tell that his father fought (and died) in the great war for freedom.

(Letter of Robert Hertz)

Dear, I recall my dreams when I was quite small, and later when a student, in the little room close to the kitchen, in the Avenue de l'Alma. With all my being I wanted to be a Frenchman, and to be regarded worthy of being a Frenchman, and to prove that I was; and I dreamed of shining deeds of war against Wilhelm. Then this desire for "integration" took another form, for my socialism was beginning to play a large part. . . .

Now the old boyish dream is born again in me stronger than ever. I am grateful to my superiors who accept me as a subordinate, to the men whom I am proud to command, these, the children of a people truly elect. Yes, I am filled with gratitude towards the country that accepts me and makes my life complete. Nothing will be too much to pay for that, and that my little son may always walk with his head high, and in the restored France not know the torment that poisoned many hours of our childhood and youth. "Am I a Frenchman? Do I deserve to be one?" No, little chap, you will have a country, and you will be able to walk the earth with a firm tread, strong in the assurance: "My papa was there, and he has given all to France." For my part, if I have need of any, it is this thought that is the sweetest recompense.

There was in the situation of the Jews, especially the German Jews newly immigrated, something dark and irregular, clandestine and bastard. I regard this war as an occasion happily come to "regularize the situation," for us and for our children. Afterwards, they can labor, if they like, in work "above" and "inter" national, but first it is necessary to show by acts that one is not "below" a national ideal. . . .

"Lettres de Prêtres aux armées." Recuillées par Victor Bucaille. Paris: Librairie Payot et Cie.

DECORATED

WHEN one of America's most illustrious citizens, an ex-president no less, received word that his son fighting with the Allied armies, had received the war Cross, it is told that he laughed aloud, not altogether for joy and pride, as we must believe, but at the thought of his tall son being kissed on both cheeks by a French general.

The Anglo-Saxon, in the matter of embraces, is a good deal like the small boy in the Barrie play who wondered how in the deuce he was going to prevent his father from kissing him upon his return from a long absence in India, and finally hit upon the ingenious device of asking his father if he did not want to see the morning paper, and thrusting it out in front of him — as a sort of bulwark. The following letter is written by a young French seminarist who was decorated (and kissed) by General Joffre:

(*Letter of Abbé G——, Decorated*)

In spite of the bad weather, Thursday was a beautiful day for me. I was at Chalons to receive the médaille militaire from the hands of General Joffre. . . . There were about fifty of us to be decorated. The generalissimo had a kind word for each one before decorating him:

"You are young to have the médaille militaire, sergeant!" he said to me.—"Twenty-three years old, my general."—"Twenty-three? Do you know I had to wait until I was sixty-three to get it? Are you pleased with it?"—"I am very proud of it, my general."—"I also." And after this brief dialogue, a big hug with two great smacking kisses.

How to tell you how I felt when the big mustaches of the general rubbed my cheeks, I do not know; at such a moment, you no longer live. Agree, that there is something very affecting for a young man of twenty-three to be embraced by this grand old man, for a sergeant to be decorated by a generalissimo. I thought for a minute that the joy and pride would turn my head. It is true that I needed only to look around me to be convinced that I am no great thing more than the others who should have received it and deserved to receive it. . . .

"Lettres du Front," par Victor Giraud. *Revue des Deux Mondes.*

ALAN SEEGER

ALAN SEEGER is the young American whose poems, with Rupert Brooke's, are among the precious things coming out of the war. The first entry in his diary, which his father found after his death in France, is dated September 27, 1914, and reads: " Fifth Sunday since enlistment." This shows that Alan Seeger wasted no time. He wrote to his mother: " I hope you see the thing as I do and think that I have done well in doing my share for the side that I think right." He entered the war with " the lightest of light hearts," and expected to return.

Alan Seeger was killed in the attack on Belloy-en-Santerre, on July 4, 1916. The last sight of him is described by a friend: " I caught sight of Seeger and called to him, making a sign with my hand. He answered with a smile. How pale he was! His tall silhouette stood out on the green of the cornfield. He was the tallest man in his section. His head erect and pride in his eye, I saw him running forward, with bayonet fixed. Soon he disappeared, and that was the last time I saw my friend. . . ."

There are bright and vivid descriptions of scene and mood in Alan Seeger's letters, since he was a poet, but it is the spirit of " the good soldier," willing to fight for what he thinks is right that gives to them their fine value. One of the letters is already famous. It belongs with the great letters of the world; with Lincoln's to the mother who lost her sons in the Civil War. It belongs in the archives not of a family alone, but of a whole proud people. Many boys after reading it must have been moved to join young Seeger's company with, as he expressed it, "the élite of the world."

(Alan Seeger's Letter)

To His Mother

MAGNEUX, June 18, 1915.

Received your letters and clippings yesterday on the march. I am not thinking of anything else but the business in hand, and if I write, it is only to divert the tedium of the trenches and to get a little intellectual exercise of which one stands so much in need now. You must not be anxious about my not coming back. The chances are about ten to one that I will. But if I should not, you must be proud, like a Spartan mother, and feel that it is your contribution to the triumph of the cause whose righteousness you feel so keenly. Everybody should take part in this struggle which is to have so decisive an effect, not only on the nations engaged, but on all humanity. There should be no neutrals but every one should bear some part of the burden. If so large a part should fall to your share, you would be in so far superior to other women and should be correspondingly proud. There would be nothing to regret, for I could not have done otherwise than what I did and I think I could not have done better. Death is nothing terrible after all. It may mean something more wonderful than life. It cannot possibly mean anything worse to the good soldier. So do not be unhappy but no matter what happens walk with your head high and glory in your large share of whatever credit the world may give me. . . .

Taken by permission from "Letters and Diary of Alan Seeger." Published by Charles Scribner's Sons.

DIXON SCOTT

LIEUTENANT DIXON SCOTT, like Rupert Brooke, died on the Gallipoli expedition. He was thirty-three years old, and had already been recognized as a sound critic and an excellent writer. Since his death, some of his articles contributed to various publications have been collected, and are an eloquent confession of loss. The list of gifted young English writers — poets, novelists and others — sacrificed to the war, is painfully long. It is not pleasant to think of brilliant young minds blotted out before they had hardly begun to throw their light. But Dixon Scott has left testimony that he made the sacrifice gladly, for posterity's sake. A paper he wrote on Rupert Brooke has become one of the memorable things that have been written about the war. The poem is prefaced by Brooke's sonnet, "The Soldier."

(Letter of Dixon Scott)

If I should die, think only this of me:
  That there's some corner of a foreign field
That is forever England   There shall be
  In that rich earth a richer dust concealed;
A dust whom England bore, shaped, made aware,
  Gave, once, her flowers to love, her ways to roam,
A body of England's, breathing English air,
  Washed by the rivers, blest by suns of home.

And think, this heart, all evil shed away,
  A pulse in the eternal mind, no less
    Gives somewhere back the thoughts by England given;
Her sights and sounds; dreams happy as her day;
  And laughter, learnt of friends; and gentleness,
    In hearts at peace, under an English heaven.
        —"The Soldier," by RUPERT BROOKE.

And these fourteen bars of beautiful melody somehow manage to cage, more completely than ever before, one of the dimmest and deepest, one of the most active and most illusive, of all the many mixed motives, beliefs, longings, ideals, which make those of us who have flung aside everything in order to fight still glad and gratified that we took the course we did. There do come moments, I must admit, when doubts descend on one dismally, when one's soldiering seems nothing but a contemptible vanity, indulged in largely to keep the respect of lookers-on. And, of course, cowardice of that sort, a small pinch of it anyway, did help to make most of us brave. There was the love of adventure, too, the longing to be in the great scrum — the romantic appeal of "The neighing steed and the shrill trump"— all the glamor and illusion of the violent thing that has figured forever in books, paintings, and tales, as the supreme earthly adventure. . . . But beneath all these impulses, like a tide below waves, there lies also a world of much deeper emotion. It is a love of peace, really, a delight in fairness and faith — an inherited joy in all the traditional graces of life, and in all the beauty that has been graced by affection. It is an emotion, an impulse, for which the word "patriotism" is a term far too simple. It is an impulse defined precisely, without suppression, blur, or excess, in the flowing lines I have quoted. One fights for the sake of happiness — for one's own happiness first of all, certain that did one not fight one would be miserable forever — and then, in the second place, for the quiet solace and pride of those others, spiritual and mental sons of ours, if not actually physical — the men of our race who will depend for so much of their dignity upon the doings of the generation before. War is a boastful, beastly business; but if we don't plunge into it now, we lower the whole pitch of posterity's life, leave them with only some dusty relics of racial honor. To enter into this material hell now is to win for our successors a kind of immaterial heaven. There will be an ease and splendor in their attitude towards life which a peaceful hand would now destroy. It is for the sake of that spiritual ease and enrichment of life that we fling everything aside now to learn to deal death.

Taken by permission from "Men of Letters," by Dixon Scott. Published by George H. Doran Company.

FERDINAND BELMONT

I met an old man at Stow-on-the-Wold
Who shook and shivered as though with cold.

And he said to me: "Six sons I had,
And each was a tall and a lively lad."

"But all of them went to France with the guns,
They went together, my six tall sons."
— WILFRID GIBSON.

FERDINAND BELMONT, called "A Crusader of France," was a young French doctor who asked to serve in the ranks. He was rapidly promoted to a captaincy, received the Cross of the Legion of Honor, and was three times cited in army orders. He was twenty-four years old when he was "killed in action." Three brothers of the young captain, called in succession, have also been killed, and the youngest brother is now serving.

His letters written to his parents are distinguished among the war letters by their spiritual quality: their philosophy and piety, and also filial devotion, perhaps to-day a little old-fashioned and provincial — except in France. To illustrate the quality of the letters and the character of the writer, Henry Bordeaux tells the story of the old Savoyard peasant who, when the news came of the death of his second son, said "God found them ready"—and went on with his plowing.

The young captain discusses the war with the clear detachment that is especially characteristic of the French. The war is horrible but to be gone through with. He draws the same distinction between the Germans and the French as Barbusse in his novel "Under Fire," and says the Germans are soldiers while the French are men. But it is the simple, absolute religious faith of the letters that gives to them their special value. This is revealed in every letter. The writer seems to have only two ideas, one to do his duty, and the other to trust God — not the Kaiser's particular friend, but " the good God, who is the God of every one." One may recall with some amusement that in 1870 Bismarck's wife sent to him a Bible, fearing he would not be able to find one in France, and marked Psalms i. 6: "The way of the ungodly shall perish."

(Letter of Ferdinand Belmont)

Ah! we have just spent a few more hard days. I have had two companies, and one of them my own, to send into action under difficult and painful conditions. The business is now over and I must thank God it did not end worse. . . .

I often think that this agitated life, full of emotions, is very enviable, and that it responds admirably to the proud ambitions of young men who would do and see everything — those who feverishly demand "to live their life," according to the common and fatal phrase.

It is true: I believe that of all this, if we survive it, we shall retain an enchanted and almost voluptuous recollection. I am sure that those who, evacuated from the front, move towards the rear, must quickly experience a feeling of dullness and mediocrity, and regret what they have left behind.

But this also may be an illusion. . . . For every life is beautiful and precious when well employed. It is not imposed events, not the frame which forms the value of an existence, but the soul which reacts and adapts itself to exterior conditions. Life is to be measured by man's capacity; circumstances in themselves signify nothing, we ourselves give them their color.

Why, therefore, say we are atoning for the inertia of preceding generations? In this immense crucible, the world, time and space are melted. Into this infinitely complex mechanism, this intricate chemical process, we are thrown atom against atom. What will come out of the whirlwind? God alone knows. But what does the knowledge of these elements so diverse and so complex matter to us? For God is there. Let us be in His hand like matter in that of the artist. Each stroke with the chisel gradually rough-hews and refines us, rids us of our original coverings and brings us towards perfection. Ah! if we only knew how to let ourselves be chiselled by our Maker. Our crime — the crime of ignorance — is that we know not how to commit ourselves to Him. It is as though the block of marble revolted against the sculptor.

What reflections the emotions of these days of war would inspire, if the days most fraught with emotions were not precisely those on which you possess the least freedom of mind! It is better so, however, for action alone can save us from ourselves.

Your letters have been, as they always are, a great comfort to me. Therefore, how I should love to merit your great affection and do something really meritorious in proof of my gratitude! But that debt I shall never pay. May God aid me to do my duty with docility and humbleness until the time He has fixed. Humility! — the great and strong and beautiful virtue.

Taken by permission from "A Crusader of France," by Captain Ferdinand Belmont. Published by E. P. Dutton & Company.

"ONE YOUNG MAN"

THE "One Young Man" of the letters collected by J. E. Hodder Williams in England is called Sydney Baxter, although this is not his real name. He is described as being, or as having been, a drab, unheroic London clerk, pale and spectacled and droop-shouldered, of the kind Wells likes to portray. Sydney Baxter was, in fact, the last man any one would expect to be a soldier. When the war came, at first he did not associate himself with it at all. It was entirely out of his world. In his office he was called "Gig-Lamps," because of his glasses. He did not know one end of a gun from another, nor the smell of powder from cologne. He knew nothing of sports of any kind until he joined the Y. M. C. A., and became an enthusiastic member of that organization. He had a mother dependent upon him — well now you know the kind.

But Sydney Baxter went to the war. Perhaps he did not "mirthfully hasten," but it did not take him long to understand that here was a case for individual responsibility; and his mother said she would "manage somehow." After nearly two years of fighting, he was wounded in nine places at the first battle of the Somme. Mr. Williams in his introduction to the letters says: "He is, as I write, waiting for a glass eye; he has a silver plate where part of his frontal bone used to be; is minus one whole finger, and the best part of a second. He is deep-scarred from his eye-lid to his hair. I can tell you he looks as if he had been through it. Well, he has."

The letter this " One Young Man " wrote to his employer telling of his " blighty," and his return to England, is said to be treasured as " the pluckiest piece of writing that has ever reached this office."

(Letter of " One Young Man ")

July 4th, 1916.

Have unfortunately fallen victim to the Hun shell in the last attack. I am not sure to what extent I am damaged. The wounds are the right eye, side of face, and left hand. They hope to save my eye, and I have only lost one finger in hand.

I will write, again, sir, when I arrive in England. At present, am near Dieppe.

Taken by permission from " One Young Man," edited by J. H. Hodder Williams. Published by George H. Doran Company.

ALEXANDER DOUGLAS GILLESPIE

BOOKS, flowers, birds, children, cats, kittens — it seems as if everything, except war, were in the letters of Douglas Gillespie — a Scotchman to be guessed by his name. His trench garden is his joy. He sends home for nasturtium seed. He wanders knee-deep in mud after violets. He transfers flowers — although " it seems a pity "—from the gardens of the ruined villages to his trench. Where others have written about the mud and the rats and the cooties, this young Scotchman writes about madonna lilies. As for the mud, he quoted one of his Highlanders: " That's the way I like ma parritch, weel thickened."

There were two Gillespie brothers, and both went to the war. At Winchester and later at Oxford, one had taken all the honors in sports, apparently, and the other in scholarship. Douglas Gillespie, according to high authority, was " one of the most distinguished men of his generation." The brother was killed in the first fighting in the pursuit at the Marne. Douglas Gillespie was killed in September, 1915, leading the charge of his men in the face of a terrific fire near La Bassée. He was the only officer to reach the German trench, where he was seen to fall. He was twenty-six.

Douglas Gillespie was one of the many young

Britishers who apparently entered the war with no hate for any one. He wrote, soon after the news from Belgrade: " I don't want to fight the Germans, for I respect them, but if the country is drawn in, I feel I must go in too, and do the best I can." But things soon happen which change his respect into horror, and make him eager to go through with it. " War at the best is a bloody business," he writes, " and it is only by sticking to the few rules that men have agreed to keep that we can prevent ourselves from descending lower than the beasts; fighting like the two devils in the ' Inferno,' who fell back into the lake of pitch biting and tearing one another with their nails."

He is soon convinced that " the traditions of all the centuries behind us " are at stake, and there must be no failure. " For if we fail, we shall curse ourselves in bitterness every year that we live, and our children will despise our memory." In his own case, there was not much chance for failure. He writes to his father: " When a man is fighting in a war like this, the news is always good if his spirit does not fail, and that I hope will never happen to your son."

In the last letter written just before the attack in which he lost his life, he finds support in the thought that so many of his friends, who have fallen in the months before, will charge in spirit by his side. His brother Tom, Rupert Brooke, G. L. Cheesman the historian, Arthur Heath, young Gladstone (" fortunate because he can give a name as well as a life for the cause he believes in "), Balfour, Marion Crawford (the novelist's son) — are some of the names appearing in the letters, with the methodical footnote, " killed in action."

(*Letter of Douglas Gillespie*)

TRENCHES, September 24, 1915.

My Dear Daddy:

Before long, I think we shall be in the thick of it, for if we do attack, my company will be one of those in front, and I am likely to lead it; not because I have been specially chosen for that, but because some one must lead, and I have been with the company longest. I have no forebodings, for I feel that so many of my friends will charge by my side, and if a man's spirit may wander back at all, especially to the places where he is needed most, then Tom himself will be here to help me, and give me courage and resource and that cool head which will be needed most of all to make the attack a success. For I know it is just as bad to run into danger as to hang back when we should push on.

It will be a great fight, and even when I think of you, I would not wish to be out of this. You remember Wordsworth's " Happy Warrior ":

> Who if he be called upon to face
> Some awful moment to which heaven has joined
> Great issues, good or bad, for human kind,
> Is happy as a lover, and is attired
> With sudden brightness like a man inspired.

Well, I never could be all that a happy warrior should be, but it will please you to know that I am very happy, and whatever happens, you will remember that.

Well, anything one writes at a time like this, seems futile, because the tongue of man can't say all that he feels — but I thought I would send this scribble with my love to you and Mother.

"Letters from Flanders," written by 2nd Lieut. A. D. Gillespie, Argyll and Sutherland Highlanders, to his home people. With an appreciation of two brothers by the Right Rev. the Bishop of Southwark. London: Smith, Elder & Co.

HARRY BUTTERS

HARRY BUTTERS, R.F.A., was a California boy who enlisted with the English army at the beginning of the war, and was killed in the fighting on the Somme at the age of twenty-four. Like Victor Chapman, he was one of fortune's favorites. He was wealthy and good looking. Not since Rupert Brooke have men and women written about any one with so much admiration and affection. Radiant, dazzling, fascinating are words used to describe him. He could drive any kind of a car, and was sure he could master a flying machine in a week; he was an expert polo player, and was all that these things imply. He went to school in England. And yet it is said that it was not because of loyalty to England, but belief in a cause in regard to the right of which he never wavered, that determined him to enter the war. He believed that the Joker, as he said, in the German deck of cards, was going to be the little word Right. He hoped that his own country would enter the war, and if it did, he would like to "get in a few licks" under the Stars and Stripes.

He had no doubts as to the ultimate outcome of the war, although he seemed to have a clear realization of what was ahead of the Allied armies. He believed in a decisive military victory over the enemy, and was impatient with the premature talk of peace.

The last thing in the world he wants to do, he says, is to die, but in one of his last letters, containing instructions what to write to his sister, he says: " Please reiterate to her how much my heart was in this great cause, and how much more than willing I am to give my life to it. Say all the nice things you can about me, but " (and this is underscored) " no lies."

In an appreciation of the " Life and Letters of Harry Butters," Mr. J. L. Garvin, editor of the *London Observer,* has picked out the one particularly choice letter, and it was not hard to choose. No letter of the war has reached a greater height of understanding and faith and high purpose. It is a remarkable letter for a boy of twenty-three to write, and puts some of the rest of us, not so clear-eyed, to shame. Mr. Garvin calls it a magnificent letter, and says it will serve on both sides of the Atlantic as the confession of faith of an American citizen in the great war. Especially the phrase, " honorable advancement of my own soul," Mr. Garvin thinks is one that should live. The letter was written after the big offensive of September, 1915:

(*Letter of Harry Butters*)

FRANCE, September, 1915.

. . . And now, just a word to reassure you, my dearest folks, and to lessen, if possible, your anxiety on my account. I am now no longer untried. Two weeks' action in a great battle is to my credit, and if my faith in the wisdom of my course or my enthusiasm for the cause had been due to fail, it would have done so during that time.

I find myself a soldier among millions of others in the great Allied Armies, fighting for all I believe to be right and civilized and humane against a power which is evil and which threatens the existence of all the rights we prize and the freedom we enjoy, although some of you in California as yet fail to realize it. It may seem to you that for me this is all quite uncalled for, that it can only mean the supreme sacrifice for nothing or some of the best years of my life wasted, but I tell you that not only am I willing to give my life to this enterprise (for that is comparatively easy, except when I think of you), but that I firmly believe if I live through it to spend a useful lifetime with you, that never will I have an opportunity to gain so much honorable advancement for my own soul, or to do so much for the cause of the world's progress, as I have here daily, defending the liberty that mankind has so far gained for himself against the attack of an enemy who would deprive us of it and set the world back some centuries if he could have his way.

I think less of myself than I did, less of the heights of personal success that I aspired to climb, and more of the service that each of us must render in payment for the right to live and by virtue of which only can we progress.

Yes, my dearest folks, we are indeed doing the world's work over here, and I am in it to the finish. "Delenda est Germania!" is our faith. "For God, for Liberty, for Honor," the call that so many have answered, if not all from as far as I.

Back me up, all of you, my nearest and dearest, and write to me often to show that you do.

Always and forever,
Most devotedly
H. A. B.

Taken by permission from "Life and Letters of Harry Butters, R.F.A." Edited by Mrs. Denis O'Sullivan. Appreciations by J. L. Garvin and Colonel Winston Churchill. Published by John Lane Company.

"A TEMPORARY GENTLEMAN"

In the first months of the war, after Mons, the Germans used to say that all the officers of the contemptible little British army had been killed, and they would not be able to produce any more. This probably explains why an English soldier signs his letters "A Temporary Gentleman," his belief apparently being that even a temporary British officer and a temporary English gentleman — like himself — who was an auctioneer's clerk before the war came and made him an aristocrat — are more than a match for "the goose-stepping Germans in the kaiser's Prussian Guard."

This "Temporary Gentleman" is the son of a widow in Brixton. He had a small sister. At fifteen, he left school and mounted a stool in the office of an auctioneer and real estate agent. In his first letter written from France he says: "I wonder if I ever should have seen it had there been no war!" Well, that, in a way, explains him. The most traveling done in his family is an annual two weeks' vacation at a seaside village. They were enjoying such a vacation when the war came and spoiled it. It was annoying. Vacations are brief and precious. But it was not long before the auctioneer's clerk had enlisted, and a little family in Brixton was entitled to a service flag with one star.

"And I used to think," he writes from the trenches, "that the pattern of my neckties made a difference to our auctions!" When he is finally wounded, he catalogues himself in the language of the auction room: "One full-size, extra heavy Temporary Officer and Gentleman; right arm and left leg slightly chipped, the whole a little shop worn, but otherwise as new. Will be sold absolutely without reserve to make room for new stock." He adds: "They have to keep as many beds as possible vacant in Clearing Stations, you know."

Of the many tributes paid to the British Tommy, the Temporary Gentleman's is one of the finest and the most sincere. He says the English soldier is the "same color all the way through," and this color he seems to think is the true blue of the genuine aristocrat:

(*Letter of " Temporary Gentleman "*)

. . . And with it all, mind you, they're so English. I mean they are kind right through to their bones; good fellows, you know; sportsmen, every one of 'em; fellows you'd trust to look after your mother. They're as keen as mustard to get to the strafing of the Boches; but that's because the Boche is the enemy, war is war, and duty is duty. You couldn't make haters of 'em, not if you paid 'em all ambassadorial salaries to cultivate a scowl and sing hymns of hate. Not them. Not all the powers of Germany and Austria could make baby killers, women slayers, and church destroyers of these chaps of ours. If I know anything about it, they are fine soldiers, but the kaiser himself —"kayser," they call him — couldn't make brutes and bullies of 'em. Warm their blood — and, mind you, you can do it easily enough, even with a football in a muddy field, when they've been on carrying fatigues all day — and, by Jove! there's plenty of devil in 'em. God help the men in front of them when they've bayonets fixed! But withal they're English sportsmen all the time, and a French child can empty their pockets and their haversacks by the shedding of a few tears.

Taken by permission from "A 'Temporary Gentleman' in France." With introductory chapters by Captain A. J. Dawson. Published by G. P. Putnam's Sons.

NORMAN PRINCE

AT the time of the visit of the French envoys to this country, at a meeting in Boston, at which Frederick H. Prince was chairman, the eloquent M. Viviani said: " I salute that young hero, Norman Prince, who has died having fought not only for France, but for America, because we have the same ideals of right and liberty."

Norman Prince was the founder of the Escadrille Americaine, later the famous Lafayette Flying Squadron, that has so chivalrously and nobly paid its country's debt to France for Lafayette and Rochambeau. Only two of the original squadron, at this writing, still live. One thinks of these young aviators, who immediately upon the outbreak of the war, volunteered their services to France, as not unlike the emblematic winged figures seen in many paintings, leading the armies, well on ahead, and pointing the way.

Norman Prince was educated abroad, and at Groton and Harvard. After being graduated with honors from the academic course at Harvard, he attended the law school. He went to Chicago to begin the practice of his profession, but was greatly interested in flying and spent much time with the Wright Brothers. He played polo and hunted and was keenly interested in every kind of sport. When the accident occurred, which resulted in his death, and both his legs were broken, he told the surgeons to be sure and not get one of his legs longer than the other, because, as his French mechanic wrote to his parents, " il faisait beaucoup le sport."

It was after an aërial raid on a German munition center that Norman Prince died from a skull fracture. He was returning from the battle in the air, and was trying to make a landing in the dark, when his machine struck a cable stretched above the trees. Both his legs were broken. The skull fracture was discovered two days later. He was not yet thirty. He won the Croix de Guerre, the Médaille Militaire, and the Croix de la Legion d'Honneur. His letters are slight, but show great devotion to the cause of the Allies, and especially to France and to his friends of the Lafayette squadron.

(*Letter of Norman Prince*)

June 26, 1916.

Dear Mama:

Poor Victor Chapman! He had been missing for a week, and we knew there was only a very remote chance that he was a prisoner. He was of tremendous assistance to me in getting together the Escadrille. His heart was in it to make ours as good as any at the front. Victor was brave as a lion and sometimes he was almost too courageous — attacking German machines whenever and wherever he saw them, regardless of the chances against him.

I have written to Mr. Chapman — a rather difficult letter to write to a heart-broken father. Victor was killed while attacking an aëroplane that was coming against Lufbery and me. Another unaccounted for German came up and brought Victor down while he was endeavoring to protect us. A glorious death — face à l'ennemi and for a great cause and to save a friend!

Your affectionate son
NORMAN.

Taken by permission from "Norman Prince." Memoir by George A. Babbitt. Published by Houghton Mifflin & Co.

VICTOR CHAPMAN

It is curious how quickly some names become legendary, and they are suddenly associated with everything that is beautiful and heroic. Rupert Brooke, the poet, had no sooner died on the Gallipoli expedition than a whole fund of story grew up about his name, which has become at once as familiar and as remotely unreal as that of some fabled knight or hero. The same is true, in hardly less degree, of Alan Seeger, the American poet in the Foreign Legion who was killed in France, and of Victor Chapman, the young American aviator who was killed at Verdun. It is easy enough to say that the "legend" grows out of youth or beauty or genius or wealth or even death, which alone transfigures. But the legend to persist, as it does with some names, must have started with truth.

The name of Victor Chapman deserves to be legendary, and his story to be told and retold, as are the stories of heroes, since it embodies the best of America. He was one of the fortunate youth. He was graduated from Harvard in 1913. He was studying at the Beaux Arts in Paris when the war broke out. He said he "guessed he would enlist." He enrolled with the Foreign Legion the first month of the war. He was a year in the trenches, and fretted at the inactivity. He wished he was in aviation. In one letter he has a plain grouch. He is sure that he will be transferred to the aviation, "just before this company goes into action and makes a brilliant attack"; or that the war will end, "just before I get my license and go to the front"— with the American Escadrille.

But luck, as he would have called it, favored him. After a brief training, he at last is able to be "doing something actively for France, instead of just toying with her expensive utensils." He was killed at Verdun, on June 23, 1916, and fell within the German lines. He was twenty-six. The story of how he met his death, plunging headlong to the rescue of his companions suddenly attacked by the German machines, and how he was carrying in his own machine a basket of oranges for a friend in the hospital, has already been told many times, and has become one of the legends.

If the character can be read in personal letters, Victor Chapman would have been the first to smile, if not to grumble, at being called a hero. Nothing could be imagined more modest and direct and simple and furthest removed from "noble" than he reveals himself in his letters—"not written for a large and admiring public, since they are not the right kind of thing." He chafes at the idea of the family worrying about him. He has the honest boy's abhorrence of a fuss. Instead of telling his people to be brave when they worry about him, he flatly tells them not to "take the edge off" from his own complete contentment in doing for the first time in his life something "worth while."

(*Letter of Victor Chapman*)

Halloween, 1915.

I get the idea that you — and Alce especially — are wearing yourselves out worrying and praying about the danger I am in, or were rather, when I was at the front, and will again when I return. It's all very parental and I appreciate it, but I wish you would not because it rather takes the edge off, and principally because it does not benefit me or any one. This is the first thing I have ever done that has been worth while, or may ever do, and you might just as well get the benefit of it without the heart-wringing worry. . . . Why not take the good and leave the bad? It is easier to pilot an aëroplane than drive an auto when you get on, and far less dangerous than the autoing I used to do daily at Cambridge. . . .

This flying is much too romantic to be real modern war with all its horrors. There is something so unreal and fairy like about it, which ought to be told by poets, as Jason's Voyage was, or that Greek chap who wandered about the Gulf of Corinth and had giants try to put him in beds that were too small for him. . . .

Every one says they get tired of flying, " It's too monotonous." I don't see it, but on the contrary, an infinite variety is this, when there is a slight sprinkling of clouds. Clouds are not thin pieces of blotting paper; but liquid, ceaselessly changing steam. I played hide-and-seek in and out them yesterday; sometimes flat blankets like melting snow on either side below me, or again, like great ice floes with distant bergs looming up, and "open water" near at hand, blue as a moonstone cloud, floating full, for all the world like gigantic jelly-fish (those that have red trailers and a sting). In the nearer pools, the mottled earth, pie-bald with sun and shadow, showed through; and it was thanks to these I knew my whereabouts. I was going from below the clouds to above them, circling in some hole; thus I realized the size and thickness of the walls,— 300 meters sheer from top to base of dazzling whiteness. Some have many feathery, filmy points and angles, others are rounded and voluminous, with cracks and caverns in them. These are all the fair-weather, fleecy clouds; for there are the lower, flatter, misty ones, and the speckled, or mare's tail clouds, above which one never reaches. There are such a lot of trumpet-shaped and wind blown clouds this evening that I should like to go out and examine them; but it's a bore for my mechanic, and I doubt if I could go high enough to warrant crossing the lines.

Your loving
VICTOR.

Taken by permission from "Victor Chapman: Letters from France," with memoir by John Jay Chapman. Published by the Macmillan Company.

ALFRED EUGÉNE CASALIS

> Under the wide and starry sky,
>   Dig the grave and let me lie.
> Glad did I live and gladly die,
>   And I laid me down with a will.
>   — ROBERT LOUIS STEVENSON'S "Requiem."

ALFRED EUGÈNE CASALIS was born on February 24, 1896, in South Africa, where his parents were missionaries. He himself intended to follow in their career, and when the war came was in the Theological Seminary at Montauban in France. He was eighteen.

He immediately began to search himself — most seriously for a boy of his years, to discover whether he has "a heart vibrating enough to fight for others, and not merely to 'save his own skin'"; whether he is quite decided to be a "champion of right, of justice, and of liberty." He says: "It is all very well to be a pacifist, but under some circumstances nothing can hold one back."

He does not wait for his class of 1916 to be called. On January 7, 1915, he writes: "I am a soldier of my own free will." He describes how he looks in a dirty and ragged uniform with the coat much too big for him — as the French soldiers' coats were likely to be, especially in the early days of the war.

His letters are full of France, of the France of

to-morrow, " the divine France that is bound to be." He is willing to die for this France. He asks for Stevenson's " Requiem," which he says he would like to translate. Like Stevenson, this French boy also wrote prayers.

He was in the general offensive at Artois in May, 1915, and was killed in a bayonet charge — a boy full of tender thoughts and piety. He was nineteen when he fell on the Field of Honor.

(*Letter of Alfred Eugène Casalis*)

For me the military life has simplified everything. Things have taken on their true values and full significance. Some difficulties which seemed insurmountable have disappeared. Intellectual sacrifices which I thought I could never accept have taken place almost of themselves, without a pang. And there results a new vitality, a desire for intense action. And then, there is always peace. However, I fear this peace both for myself and for those I love, because too often it is only human. By this I mean that it is weakness and resignation, in place of being the full consciousness of a positive duty and a real force. And I often pray as follows for myself and for those I love:

Lord, our God, our loving Father, stir up our souls in order that they may not be like stagnant waters. Do not permit us to sleep in a cowardly security, in a lifeless calm, believing that it is peace.

On the other hand, give our hearts the power to suffer intensely in communion with all grief, to revolt against all injustice, to be thrilled by the appeal of every noble and holy cause. Lord, our Christ, thy Son suffered. He wept over the death of His friend. He wept over Thy rebellious people. He wept over His work which threatened to end with His earthly life. But He lived so intensely and humanly that He was able to say to us men, " I am the life." Lord, make our hearts alive. Then will the peace descend upon them, not as the snow which numbs and freezes, but as the warmth of the sun which revives the sap in the very veins of the earth. O Lord, may thy Peace be with us; thy peace and not the peace of men. Amen.

Taken by permission from " For France and the Faith," by Alfred Eugène Casalis. Translated by Warren Edwin Bristol. Published by the Association Press.

"R. A. L.," CANADIAN STRETCHER-BEARER

And gentlemen in England now a-bed,
Shall think themselves accurs'd they were not here;
And hold their manhoods cheap whiles any speaks
That fought with us upon Saint Crispin's day.
— HENRY V.

THE interesting thing about the letters of a Canadian stretcher-bearer, "R. A. L.," are the author's own honest and changing reactions to the war. At first he is very sure he was not intended to be a soldier. But he seems to realize that somehow or other he has got to go, and join " the élite of the world." When the boys return, he is afraid " it will not be good for the chaps who stayed at home." The time comes when he is sure he will not want any of the stay-at-homes around his house! He writes this to his young wife, to whom the letters are addressed, and he adds: " My God, to think I nearly forebore to wear the khaki!"

He begins by doing orderly work in one of the base hospitals. His work as an orderly is not exactly pretty. " Can you see me doing it?" he asks, adding with pride, " and doing it right." He says: " Any one who would kick at having to wait on and work for those fellows, after what they have gone through, isn't worth much."

Finally, he cannot wait for the draft to come to him but goes to meet it. The list is full, but they take off one man and put him on. He is in the battle at Vimy Ridge. " It was the biggest day of my life." He was ahead of the tanks. The tanks were too slow for this Canadian. Each brigade went over the top of the other. He wonders what Canada thinks now. " Our splendid Canadians," indeed! The day after the battle he writes to his wife: " It is a wonderful day. Easter Monday — everybody so smiling and happy."

Alan Seeger said that after the war there would be only two kinds of men: those who had been at Verdun and those who had not. The Canadian would doubtless add — and Vimy Ridge. His letters are natural and spontaneous, slangy and boyish, manifestly honest and without " heroics." He says modern warfare is not heroic, anyway, and he even doubts if war ever was:

(Letter of " R. A. L.," Canadian Stretcher-Bearer)

This war is so " different." In any other war we might talk of " our noble cause," " the clash of arms," " death or glory," and all that kind of thing; but this one is so vast, one wee atom of a man so small, the chance for individuality coming out so remote, that it has developed, for a single Unit, into merely a job of work to be done: eat, sleep, and work. You don't fight; you can't call dodging shells, machine-gun bullets, and bombs, fighting; it's fighting all right, when you " go over." But a single battalion doesn't go over so very often, even at the Somme. I wish I could make you " get " the atmosphere. " Heroics " are dead here, a charge is not the wonderful, glorious thing we were told it was. I have even begun to wonder if it ever was, or if the poets and historians and " Press agents " of those days have been just kidding us.

No one wants to go into the trenches, yet no one (who is any one) would dodge out of it. Every one wants a soft Blighty wound, with the chance of getting to where there are no whizz bangs, and you go to bed every night. Every man I have spoken to: German, French, English, Canuck, are sick to death of it; yet to quit without a definite decision is out of the question, and no one would think of it. And how on earth am I to tell you not to worry and all that; how on earth is a husband (like me) to write to a wife (like you) about his feelings on and before going into the front line of a war like this? None of us are heroes. To read of " Our Splendid Canadians " makes us ill. We are just fed up, longing for the end, but seldom mentioning it, and hoping — when we think of it — that when we do get it — it will be an easy one, or something final. Our main effort is to think and talk as little of the war as possible. The mail is far the most important thing; the next, "What's the job to-day?" Of course newspapers are anxiously bought up — but we know the newspapers don't tell us much. And the thing is so big anyway that no one can possibly grasp even a fraction of it.

There is one new thing I've learned, and that is that it won't be good for a chap who stayed at home, when the boys return. The thing is just a bit too serious.

Taken by permission from "Letters of a Canadian Stretcher-Bearer," by R. A. L. Published by Little, Brown and Company.

"MY LITTLE NEPHEW"

THE woman author of some "Letters from France" has a number of brothers in the war, and no less than thirty-six cousins, but it is "my little nephew" who catches the imagination. He stands out heroic, stands out in a way, it may be guessed, that this young gentleman would greatly approve and enjoy. Conrad's uncle, Mr. Nicholas B., who was with Napoleon and ate the Lithuanian dog, is hardly a more gallant figure than this French boy. He is a direct descendant from D'Artagnan. To get to the front he had to run away from home and conceal himself in a military train. He was only sixteen and a half. In one of the letters we learn that the little nephew has been wounded — in both feet. He will not be crippled —" he says he is sure"; but he is "very much vexed to be wounded." And, of course, he would be! In one of the first letters to his aunt he wrote:

(*Letter from "My Little Nephew"*)

Everything here is extraordinary, and made especially to please me!

Over there the bullets whistle, the shells hum and burst: they fire off guns, and we cry out some rough language to the Boches who are entrenched twenty meters in front of us.

From time to time an aëroplane flies over our heads; the cannon bombard it and the machine guns attack it. You can imagine how I amuse myself!

Taken by permission from "Letters from France," by Jeanne le Guiner. Published by Houghton Mifflin & Company.

JEAN RIVAL

JEAN RIVAL was a Grenoble boy, the son of a college professor. He was nineteen when he fell on the field of honor. He was leading his section in an attack, and fell dead with a bullet in his head. It was Rival who led his men to the attack with the cry: "Forward, boys, with the bayonet, for the French women, our sisters!" He lies buried in Alsace, the Alsace of which he writes: "Land of Alsace that I love as dearly as my own Dauphiné!"

Like so many young Frenchmen, and youth everywhere, Jean Rival was in love with life. But he was more in love with France. In a letter written to a relative he says to tell his parents that he died "facing the enemy and protecting France with my breast." Nor does he want to be pitied. He tells his friends not to say "poor Jean," in speaking of him. He tells them to say "dear Jean," or "brave Jean," or even "little Jean," but not "poor Jean." He does not want to be pitied for doing his duty with the rest of his comrades.

Masefield, the poet, has said of France: "If all the men of France are killed, the women of France will remain. If the women of France are killed, the children of France will remain. And if the children of France must die, the dead of France will rise again." The story is told that one young French officer, in a desperate moment when all had fallen around him, cried: "Arise, ye dead men!" And the wounded struggled to their feet.

(Letter of Jean Rival)

I feel within me such an intensity of life, such a need of loving and being loved, of expanding, of breathing deeply and freely, that I cannot believe that death will touch me. Nevertheless, I well know that the rôle of commander of a company is extremely perilous; to lead men to battle is to elect oneself to be shot. Many have fallen; many will still fall. I have just heard of the death of several of my friends who only recently arrived at the front as aspirants. If this should happen to me, I count on you, my dear J——, to console my parents. You will tell them that I died facing the enemy, protecting France with my breast, and that it is not in vain that they brought me to my twentieth year, since they have given one defender to France. Tell them that my blood has not been shed in vain, and that the many and painful sacrifices of individual lives will save the life of France. . . .

"Les Diverses Familles Spirituelles de la France," par Maurice Barrès. Paris: Émile-Paul Frères.

LESLIE BUSWELL

Happy are all free peoples, too strong to be dispossessed,
But blessed are those among nations who dare to be strong
  for the rest.

BEFORE America entered the war, the American Ambulance Field Service in France, together with those who joined the Foreign Legation, represented the country's conscience. "Ambulance No. 10" is a single record, which could be multiplied many times, of the devoted service of young America to France. The driver of "Ambulance No. 10" was Leslie Buswell, a young Harvard student, who has received the coveted Croix de Guerre.

The simplicity and genuineness of these letters, the eagerness of the writer to be of service, his sympathy for the fighting men, his bewilderment at the war and horror of its cruelties — all make them memorable. An example of his earnestness is seen in the letter describing a dinner in the trenches on the French fête day of July 14, when he was asked to sing the American national anthem, and "got up and did so as loud and as heartily as I knew how."

"Ambulance No. 10" operated in the neighborhood of the much fought over Bois-le-Prêtre, and carried about 7,500 wounded a month; steady driving considering the capacity of the "little cars."

In one letter, the author writes, "I carried over forty wounded yesterday a distance of one hundred and sixty kilos." And in another letter, he says:

(*Letter of Leslie Buswell*)

. . . It was a sad trip for me — a boy of about nineteen had been hit in the chest and half his side had gone — "tres pressé," they told me — and as we lifted him into the car, by a little brick house that was a mass of shell holes, he raised his sad, tired eyes to mine and tried a brave smile. I went down the hill as carefully as I could and very slowly, but when I arrived at the hospital I found I had been driving a hearse, and not an ambulance. . . .

It made me feel pretty bad — the memory of that faint smile which was to prove the last effort of some dearly beloved youth. All the poor fellows look at us with the same expression of appreciation and thanks; and when they are unloaded, it is a common thing to see a soldier, probably suffering the pain of the damned, make an effort to take the hand of the American helper. I tell you tears are pretty near sometimes.

Taken by permission from "Ambulance No. 10," by Leslie Buswell. Published by Houghton Mifflin & Co.

WILLIAM YORKE STEVENSON

ONE of the heroes of the war is the " little car." It has become endowed with a kind of personality. All the ambulance drivers write affectionately of their " flivver," their " Tin Lizzie," their " Henry," as they variously call it. In the Foreign Legion every man is supposed to have a comrade de combat who always goes with him into action. The little car is the ambulance driver's comrade de combat.

The little car has been decorated with the Croix de Guerre. When the famous Section I of the American Ambulance service was to receive the Croix de Guerre, the French general bestowing the decoration announced that since the section had no regimental standard, he would " decorate " the car. " It was a flivver! " says William Yorke Stevenson. " Just a plain flivver, the after overhang of which gave the outfit the graceful aspect of an overfed June bug." The Croix de Guerre is in the top corner of the flag; an eagle is in the center; there are three stars, indicating the number of times the section has been cited; and there are the names: Ypres, Dunkerque, Somme, Verdun, Argonne, Aisne — a proud record for the little car.

William Yorke Stevenson, of Philadelphia, drove the famous Ambulance No. 10 in 1915, on the Somme and at Verdun. This is one of the ten first American ambulances of the American Field Service, the gift of a New York woman in 1915, and driven by Leslie Buswell in that year at Pont-à-Mousson. Ambulance No. 10 is no longer in the service. It is invalided. Mr. Stevenson thinks it should not be permitted to end on a scrap heap, but should be preserved in a museum.

Mr. Stevenson was financial editor of a Philadelphia newspaper, when early in 1916 he went to France and volunteered in the ambulance service. He has been in command of the celebrated Section I, and has himself received the Croix de Guerre. He says when he first went to France, the deeper and more serious aspects of the war did not particularly appeal to him. But, later on, he writes, "France gets a sort of grip on you, and one begins to want to stay and see it through."

(Letter of William Yorke Stevenson)

> For history's hushed before them,
> And legend flames afresh;
> Verdun, the name of thunder
> Is written on their flesh.
> — LAURENCE BINYON.

July 2, 1916.

The Germans made an attack near Vaux and our " tir de barrage " stopped it. We drove past some one hundred guns, " 75's " and " 105's," whose muzzles project over the road, and when they fire as we pass in an incessant " tir rapide," the noise is enough to break the ear-drums. I stuff cotton in my ears and keep my mouth open. The sheets of flame come half across the road, and the concussion has even broken some of the windows in the cars. . . . The "tir de barrage" is alone worth crossing the ocean to see. A solid line of flame several kilometers long, crowned by exploding shrapnel and all kinds of colored lights and flares and a noise so deafening as to make one's head reel and one's brain stop working. There were eleven hundred guns working just as fast as they could (about twenty-five shots a minute) for an hour in the space of about two square miles. No words of mine can do justice to that "tir de barrage" across the Étain road. I have been scared in my life, but never like that. The German "incomers" one regards as luck. One hears the warning whistle and thinks it's coming right at one, and it falls one hundred yards away. Again one hears the whistle and regards it as distant — and she blows up right beside one. There's a cheerful uncertainty that means bad luck if one's hit; but when obliged to drive in front, within twenty feet, of those 75's, and others, with the flame apparently surrounding you, and unable to hear or think for the stunning noise, you don't know whether the motor is going, and you also wonder where the wads are going. They alone are enough to kill a man. You also hope the gunners are on to their job, as some new recruit might aim a foot too low! Then, occasionally, a badly timed shot bursts at the muzzle, which means exactly above the car. Believe me, I'd rather take a chance with the erratic " Germ " incomers than to have to pass that often. If I get out of this without being permanently deaf, I'll be lucky.

Taken by permission from " At the Front in a Flivver," by William Yorke Stevenson. Published by Houghton Mifflin & Co.

"CAMION LETTERS"

No picture of the great war has appealed more to the imagination and given a better idea of its gigantic operations than the unending procession of the huge army trucks, crawling like a mammoth caterpillar over muddy, deeply rutted and continually shell-swept roads; traveling at night without lights, and carrying night and day munitions and food and other supplies to the army. The transport service has been called the backbone of the army. If this is so, it is interesting to know that some American college men have been a very important part of this backbone.

The first American flag authorized to be borne in the war was carried by a unit of college men, most of them from Cornell University, in the first transport section of the American Field Service in France. With the exception of the aviators, the college men were the first armed American force in Europe. They originally volunteered for the ambulance service. But when they arrived in France, instead of the little cars, they were asked to drive the big five-ton munition trucks instead, which the French call "camions."

Although it was not unlike agreeing to buy a Thrift Stamp and being asked to subscribe to a Liberty Bond instead, almost without exception, the men willingly agreed to the transfer, and regarded it only as that " bit more," expressed by one of them who, when writing home of his promotion, said: "I want you to know how lucky I am and that so far I've done my duty and that bit more which counted." The general feeling appears to have been that anything that France wanted had to be done. "After my experience with the submarine," one of the boys writes, "and learning practically at first hand the enemy that not only France, but the United States, has to deal with, and seeing the tremendous sacrifice going on about me without quailing, I feel that any sacrifice of personal desires that I make is infinitely trivial."

Although most of the camion drivers are very young, young enough to have an inordinate appetite for chocolate, apparently, and a great desire for a mouth organ, the issues of the war are clear to them. One of the most serious of the " Camion Letters " expresses an abhorrence of war equal to the most unyielding pacifist's. But this is the very simple and not at all complex reason why he is glad that his country is in the struggle which it is hoped will end militarism and its evils forever. The writer of the letter is R. A. Browning, of Cornell:

(*Camion Letter*)

Paris, May 6, 1917.

What has impressed me most during my short stay here is the earnestness of the French people in the present conflict; their willingness to sacrifice everything for the great cause which they have been upholding since the beginning of the war. . . .

It is indeed a great consolation to me now, more so than I ever imagined it would be, to know that the United States is at last a participant in this awful affair. It is indeed a miserable affair and a pity that the whole world should be required to turn from the ordinary pursuits of life and peace to those of war. But for a long time a war against oppression, crime, and frightfulness has been waged for us, and we have reaped the " benefits " in money.

Thank God we can now lift up our heads and square our shoulders again! The Stars and Stripes again mean what it meant in '76 and '12 and '61 — it stands for honor and peace and humanity even though the price be war. I long for the day when our first American troops land in France to fight shoulder to shoulder with the rest of the world against selfishness and greed; and when this war is over, as I pray it soon will be, may America, my country, take the initiative in the movement for an alliance of nations, a world federation so organized that war will no longer be possible. Do not think that mine is a schoolboy patriotism. I despise a fight as such; I despise war — as such. We — the United States — are fighting against war, not for it.

Taken by permission from " Camion Letters." Introduction by Martin W. Sampson. Published by Henry Holt and Company.

A FRENCH MRS. BIXBY

Mrs. Bixby was the mother of five sons, who, as Lincoln wrote in his treasured letter, died gloriously on the field of battle. There is a French mother, however, who having already lost eight sons in the war, sent forth the last. Her letter should become as famous as Lincoln's. The boy's sisters wrote the letter to him, at their mother's dictation. Like the old woman in the Synge play, it would seem that with all her sons gone this French mother too might at last sleep o' nights.

(Letter of a French Mrs. Bixby)

I hear that Charles and Lucien were killed on the twenty-eighth of August. Eugene is seriously wounded. As for Louis and John, they are dead also. Rose is missing. Mamma weeps. She says for you to be brave and go to avenge them. I hope your chief will not refuse to let you do this. John had the Legion of Honor. Succeed him. They have all been taken from us. Out of eleven who went to the war, eight are dead. My dear brother, do your duty. One only asks this of you. God has given your life to you; he has the right to take it back. It is Mamma who says this.

Thy Sisters.

"Lettres du Front," by Victor Giraud. Revue des Deux Mondes.

A LITTLE MOTHER

Hélène Payeur is the name of the writer of the following letter. She is fifteen. Her father, until he joined the colors, was a forestry guard in the neighborhood of Raon. Hélène became separated from her mother, and was alone with her little sister, aged seven, and her brother, aged five, in the storm center of a great battle. It was a month before the mother was able to rejoin the little family. But how it " managed " is told in the letter:

(*Letter of a Little Mother*)

Forestry House of Cenimont
near Sainte-Barbe.

Monsieur:

I am hurrying to answer your letter which I have received with pleasure. I may tell you that we are all home. Mamma, from whom we were separated in the battle of August 25, returned on September 21; she had been as far as Soutenay. As for me, I went as far as Sainte-Barbe with her, there I remained a day and a night, until the German troops arrived. We carried off our best linen and our cow. When Sainte-Barbe was burned, they insisted upon letting the cow burn too, and would not let me save it.

I was alone with Rita and Robert for an hour, during which time they never stopped crying. You could not hear each other because of the noise of the cannon and the bullets. The Germans wanted to keep me from going through, but finally permitted me on account of the children.

I reached Baccarat on the other side of the forest. But a battle starts up, and I fall on the ground from fear of the bullets. I kept on going, in spite of the refusal of the Germans. I reached la Chapelle when a big battle broke out, beyond Thiaville. I went on all the same. I arrived at the house and found it completely looted. I immediately started in to clean it, in order to be able to stay in it. I had nothing to eat, but finally the Prussians returned to get their dinner at our house, and made us eat with them. They had our other cow killed. It was a nuisance, for our cow was in the stable, and the horse was hidden in the ditch at the end of the road. It was necessary for me to hide all that in being cross-examined by the officers. They took our rye and our corn, which was not yet cut. They forbade me to bring it in. They took all our underwear for their wounded and we have nothing to put on. Rita and Robert are going barefoot. They took all our potatoes, and I had nothing to say.

I was anxious because I did not know where Mamma was. All is sad at this time for us, because we have to work hard with no pay. It is three months since I have seen a sou. Finally, if I told you all, I should never be done.

We have had news of Papa, and he tells us that he is well; but he does not tell us where he is. Mamma saw him at Gicourt, when he left for the north.

As for the little hunting lodge, nothing is left but the fireplace; the windows are broken, and there are many German graves all about. We have still some bedding, but happily because we hid it in the forest with a feather bed. The forestry house is burned, also that of Miclo and of Marchal.

Our little dog has disappeared, and we do not know what was his end. . . .

"L'Âme française et la guerre," par Maurice Barrès. Paris: Émile-Paul Frères.

JEAN GIRAUDOUX

NOTHING was too good for a French soldier in those first thrilling days in August, 1914, when Mulhouse (not Mulhausen) was in the headlines, and the French flew towards the lost provinces like homing pigeons. In front of every doorstep stood pails of wine and sweet drinks and baskets of food. There were flowers for every man and gun. The doors of the houses stood wide open, even at the back, so you could see right through, writes Lieutenant Jean Giraudoux. It was a time of great joy and great emotion. The little children " adore us," and cry " Vive la France," in a throaty fashion —" as if it hurt." But it is to the French women, who made a living hedge all along the line of route, to whom their gallant countryman pays an interesting tribute:

(*Letter of Jean Giraudoux*)

O French women of the railway stations, how you all are remembered! All along our route, at every stop of the train, absolutely belonging to us, the slaves of each one of us, running from the railroad track to the town — that was down hill — to fill twenty canteens, which were empty when they took them and weighed twenty kilos on their return — that was up hill; not able to keep from giving two pieces of chocolate to every man — instead of one — and in despair at having twice run out too soon of their supply; bourgeoises, peasants, little girls with their English governesses — radiant, freed since yesterday of a frightful doubt in regard to England — all passing in and out of our lives as people in the lives of famous travelers: the teacher, every one of whose pupils had written and signed a little letter of good cheer for the soldiers; the butcher's wife, whose stock was sold out, who thought suddenly of her jams, and flew to her cupboards; dark young girls, thin, devoured by the war, at a mining station, who changed for us the first five franc note, this French money that they had planned to keep always as a souvenir; the shy cousins who noiselessly half opened the door of our silent car, about two o'clock in the morning, and trembled with joy to see it suddenly awake, jump out on the graveled platform, bury in knapsacks the chocolate, of which they proudly named the brand, because it was so dark; fair statue, with the golden head, who scrutinized and recognized each face, and refused to give me a second glass of wine, when I stood in the line again; the wife, who looked on at the others, without helping, under the shining acacias, helpless in her grief, yet who wanted to see us, and at first refused to tell us, whether because of her agony or fear, her husband's regiment, and sobbing aloud when it was at last confessed — a living hedge of women, right up to the frontier, all within a few yards of us — except the young girl of Montceaux who would never come near — rising above the track of the train, rising above their own lives, above their own modesty, ready also to die — and defying the fast express. . . .

"Retour d'Alsace," par Jean Giraudoux. Paris: Émile-Paul Frères.

YVONNE X——

IF there are any who feel horror at the thought of young French boys charging with fixed bayonets, and shouting: " Forward! forward! with the bayonet, for the French women, our sisters! " they should read the story of Yvonne X——.

Yvonne was one of the many thousands of girls deported from Lille to do agricultural work for the Germans. Consistent with their eminent frankness and fairness, the Germans announced the deportations in advance. The inhabitants of Lille were warned not to leave their homes between eight o'clock in the evening and six in the morning. (The shameful work was appropriately to be done in the dark.) The people were told to prepare their baggage of linen and blankets and kitchen utensils, weighing so many pounds. And finally they were benevolently advised to obey orders and " remain calm! "

Yvonne X—— was one of the forty-eight of the 6000 young women deported from Lille, whom the German government finally charitably permitted to return to their homes, after the whole world had risen in horror at the abominable thing that had been done. She kept a diary, which was printed in the *Revue des Deux Mondes*. Some of it is hardly quotable. After traveling in cattle cars, and arriving at their destination, the girls were not immediately turned into the fields to do the alleged necessary planting. On the contrary, some of the girls, the better looking ones, were taken before medical officers, stripped and vilely inspected. When they protested against the "work" that they then learned was to be assigned to them, they were told again to be "calm" and not make a fuss, since they were "all French and all alike." Those who were put to work in the fields were lashed when they halted in their labors. They were starved. Yvonne's story of how the Germans, in their methodical selection of those who were to be deported, street by street, finally halted before her own door, is dramatic:

(*Letter of Yvonne X———*)

... At four o'clock, I awoke with a start. They were ringing at the door of our neighbors. Mamma, with whom I share a room, jumped out of bed. "Here they are!" Mamma had scarcely said the words, when, under our windows, we heard the noise of boots and the tap-tap of rifle butts on the pavement. Our bell rang furiously. Shall we refuse to open? Impossible. By order of the military government, one must always open to Germans. If one refuses, there is punishment or prison. My mother goes down stairs. She finds herself confronted by seven soldiers. "Madame, how many persons live here?" "Three: myself, my two daughters." A soldier consults the list of people in the house that has to be posted in every corridor. "Show them, madame." But before Mamma was able to prevent him, the Boche enters my room. I was still in bed. The man asks me: "Are you Mademoiselle Genevieve?" "Yvonne," corrects Mamma. "Mademoiselle, get up! The officer will be here in five minutes." . . . The five minutes are hardly passed, when the officer arrives. Ten men accompany him, with fixed bayonets. . . . "You have twenty minutes to get ready." . . . The twenty minutes are barely up, when the soldiers' rifle-butts are heard in the vestibule, and they shout up in a loud voice: "Mademoiselle, hurry up! hurry up! It is time to go." Mamma blesses me. "Be brave, my child, try to comfort those around you." We kissed each other, and parted without tears. . . .

"Emmenées en esclavage, pour cultiver la terre. Journal d'une déportée," par H. Célarie. Revue des Deux Mondes.

CHARLES PÉGUY

Charles Péguy was the idol of young France. For many years he was the editor of *Les Cahiers de la Quinzaine,* a unique publication in Paris, printing literary, political and documentary works as separate books; in the *Cahiers* originally appeared Romain Rolland's long serial novel, "Jean Christophe."

Péguy was also a poet. He was the son of a workingman and the grandson of peasants, and his faithfulness to the soil of his ancestors, Pierre de Lanux says, " was like France's herself." Maurice Barrès says of Péguy that his whole life was " an assault on the German positions."

Péguy went gayly off to the war as a lieutenant of reserve with his section of infantry. He was killed at the Battle of the Marne, and thus is named with those heroes who in September, 1914, saved Paris and France and perhaps the world. For a lieutenant, he was "a chic type," one of his men said of him. He had no fear. His death, as described by one of his men, is cited in France as an example of how her heroes die:

(*The Death of Charles Péguy*)

The young and clear voice of Lieutenant Péguy directs the fire; he is standing behind us, courageous under the shower of shrapnel, cadenced to the infernal tap-tap of the Prussian machine-guns.

This terrible race through the oats has taken our breath away, sweat drowns us, and our brave lieutenant is in the same predicament. A brief moment of respite, then his voice trumpets to us, "Advance!"

Ah! this time it is no laughing matter. Climbing the slopes, and lying flat on the ground, bent double, in order to offer less target to the bullets, we rush to the attack! The terrible harvest continues, frightful; the song of death hums around us. The hundred meters are thus made; but to go further for the moment, it is madness, a general massacre, not more than ten of us will arrive! Captain Guerin and the other lieutenant, M. de Cornillière, are killed dead. "Lie down!" cries Péguy, "and fire freely!" but he himself remains standing, field glasses in his hand, directing our fire, heroic in the inferno.

We shoot like madmen, black with powder, the gun burning the fingers. At each moment there are cries, groans, significant death rattles; dear friends fell at my side. How many are dead? One counts no longer.

Péguy is always standing, in spite of our cries to "Lie down!" glorious madman, in his bravery. The most of us no longer have any sand bags, lost at the time of the retreat, and a bag at this time is a precious shelter. And the voice of the lieutenant keeps on crying: "Shoot! Shoot! For God's sake!" Some complain: "We have no bags, Lieutenant; we shall all be killed!" "That doesn't matter. Neither have I any bag, do you see? Keep on firing!" And he stands up as if to defy the shrapnel, seeming to summon the death that he glorified in his verse. At the same time a murderous bullet crashes the head of this hero, shatters his noble and beautiful countenance. He fell without a cry, having had, in the recoil of the barbarians, the ultimate vision of a near victory; and when, one hundred meters farther on, I take a wild look back, I see down there a black spot in the midst of so many others, stretched lifeless, on the warm and dusty ground, the body of this hero, of our dear lieutenant.

"Avec Charles Péguy," par Victor Boudin. Paris: Librairie Hachette.

LOUIS KEENE

LOUIS KEENE is another of "those Canadians," one of the 3,500 Canadian volunteers, who enlisted in the first days of the war, and were in England before the Germans could say their equivalent for Jack Robinson. Louis Keene is an artist. He was sketching with his father in Canada, when he was sent for by a Toronto paper to return to make war cartoons. But it was not long before he was over there, and the captain of a machine-gun section, and, as we must believe, an artist at that job, too.

In a description of No Man's Land, he quotes from the diary of a German soldier, killed at Hooge, in August, 1915. He wonderingly says of the German: "He was writing his diary at the same time I was writing mine." They were both in the sharp fighting around the salient at Ypres.

(Letter of Louis Keene)

A trip to No Man's Land is an excursion you never forget. It varies in width and horrors. My impression was similar to what I should feel being on Broadway without my clothes — a naked feeling. Forty-seven and one-half inches are necessary to stop a bullet, and it's nice to have that amount of dirt between you and the enemy's bullets. The dead lie out in between the lines or hang up on the wire; they don't look pretty after they have been out some time. It's a pleasant job to have to get their identification disks, and we have to search the enemy dead for papers and even buttons so that we can know what unit is in front of us. . . .

I managed to get a diary kept by a German soldier who fell on the field. It gives the point of view of a man in the trenches on the other side of the line. He was writing his diary at the same time I was writing mine. . . .

"July 17th. Marched to new quarters. We have got a new captain. He wants to see the company, so at 8 A.M. drill in pouring rain. Four times we have to lie on our belly and get wet through and through. All the men grumbling and cursing. At eleven we are dismissed, I, with a bad cold and a headache. I wish this soldiering were over.

"August 4th. At every shot, the dug-outs sway to and fro like a weather-cock. This life we have to stick to for months. One needs nerves of steel and iron. Now I must crawl into a hole, as trunks and branches of trees fly in our trench like spray.

"August 6th. The smoke and thirst are enough to drive one mad. Our cooker doesn't come up. The 126th give us bread and coffee from the little they have. If only it would stop! We get direct hits one after another and lie in a sort of dead end, cut off from all communication. What a feeling to be thinking every second when I shall get it. —— has just fallen, the third man in the platoon. Since eight the fire has been unceasing: the earth shakes and we with it. Will God ever bring us out of this fire! I have said the Lord's prayer and am resigned. . . ."

Taken by permission from "Crumps," by Louis Keene. Published by Houghton Mifflin & Co.

CAPTAIN GILBERT NOBBS

IN a preface to a book describing his war experiences, Captain Gilbert Nobbs, plucky Britisher, says: "This is my first book. It is also my last." He is blind.

Captain Nobbs was five weeks on the firing line. For four weeks he was mourned as dead, and later received a bill from his solicitor "for services regarding the death of Captain Nobbs." Three months he was a prisoner of war in Germany.

The British captain was leading his men in a charge when catastrophe overwhelmed him. He was yelling to his men: "Get ready to charge, they are running. Come on! Come on!" He jumped out of the shell hole, and his men followed. He was hit in the head. The bullet emerged through the center of his right eye. The optic nerve of the other eye was affected. He was blind.

At the same time he says he did not lose consciousness. But he had an odd experience, in which he went down into the valley and came back. Call it an hallucination, a trick of the brain, or what we will. Captain Nobbs merely records the incident. His own belief, he says, he will keep to himself. But whatever it was, for him there is no longer any mystery about death; nor does he dread it.

He insists that he does not deplore the loss of his sight, and that he can say in all sincerity that he was never happier in his life. His head may be bloody, but it is unbowed. And he is alive!

(Letter of Captain Gilbert Nobbs)

Even the loss of God's great gift of sight ceases to become a burden or affliction in comparison with the indescribable joy of life snatched from death.

There are men, and we know them by the score, who are constantly looking out on life through the darkened windows of a dissatisfied existence; whose conscience is an enemy to their own happiness; who look only on the dark side of life, made darker by their own disposition.

Such men, and you can pick them out by their looks and expression, who build an artificial wall of trouble, to shut out the natural paradise of existence; these men who juggle with the joy of life until they feel they would sooner be dead, do not know, and do not realize the meaning of life and death with which they trifle.

Let us think only of the glory of life; not of the trivial penalties which may be demanded of us in payment, and which we are so apt to magnify until we wonder whether the great gift of life is really worth while.

Let us not think of our disadvantages but of those great gifts which we are fortunate enough to possess; let us school ourselves to a high sense of gratitude for the gifts we possess, and even an affliction becomes easy to bear.

Here I am, thirty-six years of age, in the pride of health, strength, and energy, and suddenly struck blind.

And what are my feelings? Even such a seeming catastrophe does not appall me. I can no longer drive, run, or follow any of the vigorous sports, the love for which is so persistent in healthy manhood. I shall miss all these things, yet I am not depressed.

Am I not better off, after all, than he who was born blind? With the loss of my sight, I have become imbued with the gift of appreciation. What is my inconvenience compared with the affliction of being sightless from birth?

For thirty-six years I had become accustomed to sights of the world and now, though blind, I can walk in the garden on a sunny day; and my imagination can see it and take in the picture.

I can talk to my friends, knowing what they look like, and by their conversation read the expression on their faces. I can hear the traffic of a busy thoroughfare, and my mind will recognize the scene.

I can even go to the play; hear the jokes and listen to the songs and music, and understand what is going on without experiencing that feeling of mystery and wonder which must be the lot of him who has always been blind.

And the greatest gift of all, my sense of gratitude, that after passing through death, I am alive!

Taken by permission from "On the Right of the British Firing Line," by Captain Gilbert Nobbs. Published by Charles Scribner's Sons.

WOUNDED

M. Maurice Barrès, who since the beginning of the war has been almost a postoffice department in himself in collecting and preserving the letters of the French soldiers, quotes the following letter written by a little Frenchman, so young, as he says, as hardly to be more than a child. M. Barrès seems to like this letter particularly, possibly because of its mention of Déroulède —" cet ancien " as the youngster calls him — and of Lorraine. M. Barrès is himself from Lorraine, and he often takes delight in writing Lorraine-Alsace instead of the usual way. As much as to the Louvre or Notre Dame or Napoleon's tomb, or any of the other sights of Paris, tourists flock to see the statue of Strasbourg in the Place de la Concorde, always with the mourning wreaths heaped about its base — which, according to this little Parisian, are to be changed to palms of glory:

(Letter of a Wounded)

Papa has already written me of having seen you and told you the news about me. How I should like to have been in his place and told you myself, for I am sure that he will have exaggerated the little I have done. Papa is proud of having his son wounded. But he is not as proud as I am. If you knew how it gave me a sensation of pain, but, if I can so express it, of happy pain. I was glad to be wounded, I, who dreamed so often of suffering a little for France, and the thought gave me strength, the will to get well as soon as possible, in order to go back to rejoin my comrades who are still fighting.

Do you know, it bores me to be inactive, I still have the thirst for battle. I must still have my little revenge, apart from the great revenge which we are all in the way of preparing. . . . How one has a good conscience and a tranquil spirit while feeling the bullets and the shells flying around one, and saying to oneself: "It is for France!" One must be on the battlefield to see how well she is defended, how all her children meet and fight with a song on their lips, courage in their hearts. It is so beautiful to feel this great patriotic breeze pass over you, and when the tri-color is unfolded, one no longer lives, one runs to meet death. It rushes like a hurricane past you, and one finds oneself marveling, transformed: one is a man, one is a Frenchman.

Ah! We shall soon have with us again our Alsace-Lorraine brothers, and we shall no longer go to the statue of Strasbourg to place mourning wreaths there, but palms of glory and of gratitude. Alas! Déroulède will be missing. But it doesn't matter. He knew how to make thousands of Déroulèdes, the beautiful youth of France, and in souvenir of " this elder," we have given ourselves body and soul to France.

God and France! Here is our motto. The one protects us, and we defend the other. Is it not a glorious mission? And if by chance I should be left on the battlefield, think of a little Frenchman, a little Parisian, who surrendered his soul, happy in the thought of a greater France!

"L'Âme française et la guerre," par Maurice Barrès. Émile-Paul Frères, éditeurs. Paris.

HUMPHREY COBB

WHEN he was nineteen, and before America entered the war, Humphrey Cobb, of New York, went abroad to serve with the English army in France. He was born in Italy and lived there until he was fourteen, although when he was nine he started going to an English school. It was his feeling for his school and his friends over there that made him eager to help in the Allied cause. He enlisted in Canada.

Some of Humphrey Cobb's letters are amusingly young — and some are alarmingly old. In one letter, he is begging for sporting sheets and baseball scores, and in another is telling gravely of things perhaps no boy, as Kipling says of Dicky Hatt — in " The Pride of His Youth "— should be expected to know.

Humphrey Cobb's letters are written to his mother. Almost every letter expresses a great contentment at being in the war. He seems to know that the war is the big event of his generation, and he writes that those who will have missed it will always be " out of it." In his last letter, written just before starting for France, he says: " What I would have missed, if I had not enlisted!" The following letter was written from a training camp in England:

(*Letter of Humphrey Cobb*)

July 17, 1917.

... You know, mother, sometimes I can hardly believe that I am in England again; England where every spot is historic and the whole land is beautiful. England, a great camp of soldiers, a nation at war, the heart of the world. And it seems strange to think that below the horizon is glorious, magnificent France; and beyond her beautiful Italy — the land of poetry, art and love.

Good God, mother, what an experience this is! What men I run up against and get to know! What stories of roving lives I have heard. What tragedies and comedies I have seen, and into what lives and characters I have had a glimpse. And even this is child's play to what we will see, hear and experience in France. Thank God, I have not missed it! It is all big, mother, nothing petty or small. And the greatest thing of this life is its perpetual and recurrent humor. How blue we all get. How happy we are, how we swear, how we laugh. I wish you could have seen our hut this morning, when the news came up that some other hut had taken our breakfast as well as theirs. " Well, I'll be damned if I'll go on parade or work if I don't get fed!" was about all you could hear, and the funny part of it was they all went on parade the same as usual and lived through it in spite of threats to drop dead in the ranks from lack of food. They won't do this, and they won't do that, but they always do it when the time comes.

. . . One request — about the end of September and the beginning of October the world's series will begin — that is baseball games between the leading teams of the American and National League. If you can find out when they begin will you save all the sporting sheets of every day during the series, but should you overlook them, as your inexperience in the sporting pages might lead you to do, just get the scores from some one, Uncle—— or Uncle ——, and they will tell you which came out on top and that will do just as well.

Communicated.

EDMUND YERBURY PRIESTMAN

THE story of Edmund Yerbury Priestman reflects glory on the Boy Scouts. He was a young Scoutmaster in Sheffield, England, who received his commission in October, 1914. His letters are published under the title " With a B. P. Scout in Gallipoli." He died at Suvla Bay. He died defending an advanced post for which he had volunteered. It was the kind of an advanced post in which the men run forward, at night, with sandbags, and try to dig themselves in before the enemy's guns can reach them. In this case the Turks rushed the position. Lieutenant Priestman did not retire, but opened fire, and held the enemy back for a time, until a second rush, when the little band was overcome. The entire lot, thirty of them, was wiped out clean as a slate. The position so heroically defended has been named " Priestman's Post."

Edmund Priestman was twenty-five when he was killed. His letters are boyish and full of fun, and are illustrated with his own sketches, which are clever and humorous. The spirit of the letters is indicated in the incident when two of the subalterns " thought it was one of our party and so were prepared to jeer." If the motto of the Boy Scouts is " for life or death Be Prepared," surely the motto for the young Englishman at war is " for life or death be prepared to jeer and be jokey." But young Priestman also had his serious moment and a fine talent for descriptive writing as seen in the following letter:

(*Letter of Edmund Yerbury Priestman*)

A Trench,
August 27th, 1915.

The small boy who used to try and say the twenty-third Psalm all in one breath never guessed that he would ever experience what that "Valley" really could be like; but having spent two hours in it last Saturday afternoon, he's going to try and describe his experiences.

You must try and imagine us (at about the time many of your local "knuts" were leaving for the cricket-ground or golf links) squatting on our haunches in a shallow and dusty trench, listening to the most appalling uproar you could dream of. Behind us our big guns are roaring, above us the shells are tearing through the air, and in front of us, all up the long valley ahead, the crash of their bursting is simply deafening. Somewhere (all too vaguely described to us) are three lines of Turkish trenches which must be taken to-day. . . .

Can you picture the feeling of all of us as we watch the minute-hand slowly creep towards three? Ten minutes only now. Now only seven. And what of us all when that hand shall have touched the half hour . . . ? The dentist's grisly waiting den, the ante-room to the operating theater — these multiplied a thousandfold in their dread anticipation.

And now the moment has come. A whistle sounds — a scramble over the trusty parapet we have learned to know as a shield for so many hours, and the valley is before us. "Whiss! whissss!" The air is full on every side with invisible death. "Whisss! phutt!" A bullet kicks up a little spray of dust from the dry gray earth underfoot, another and another to left and right. The sensation of terror is swallowed up in an overwhelming conviction that the only possible course is forward — forward at any cost. That is what we have been telling ourselves all through the long waiting, and that is our only clear impression now. Forward — and we instinctively bend as one does to meet a hailstorm, and rush for it.

Beyond the rough plowed ground over which we are advancing lies a low, thick belt of brambles and bushes. Here, for a time, we can lie under cover and regain our breath for a second rush. The man on my left stumbles and comes down with a crash and a groan. Only an instinctive catch of the breath, and the old conviction — forward at all costs — swamps all other sensations.

Down we go behind the kindly shelter and "Whisss! whisss!" the bullets flow over us. . . .

... Two more rushes over the open and I find only three of my men left to follow me. The others are not all hit, of course; many have got isolated with other parties. We are all wondering where on earth we are by now, as we've certainly advanced quite seven hundred yards, and no trench yet!

Finally, a rush takes us into a long narrow ditch where we are safe from the bullets. ...

Dusk is falling, and we are preparing to spend the night in our safe retreat when a rustling comes from up the ditch. I grip my rifle and prepare for action. The sound comes nearer and I challenge it. "Friend," comes the feeble reply, and down the trench there crawls what was once — only a few hours ago — a man, and now. ... It is hard to tell the poor fellow that I can do nothing for him, but he is beyond all help now and he knows it. A drink of water helps matters and he lies back, as comfortable as I can make him, and asks quietly for a "woodbine!" Oh, you splendid British Tommy — not even to be daunted by those hideous explosive bullets we all know so well by now — there must be some Power behind you that lends you who suffer courage and we who have "come through" the conviction that such courage can only be on the side of right and justice.

As night falls, it is decided that I should take a message back to the Brigadier to report where our party is dug in, so I slip my revolver into my pocket

nd set out. . . . That's the whole story. What
ve gained and lost that day form no part of it —
he papers will show all that some time. . . .

Taken by permission from "With a B. P. Scout in Gallipoli," by Edmund Yerbury Priestman. Published by E. P. Dutton & Co.

THE MARSEILLAISE

Allons, enfants de la patrie,
Le jour de gloire est arrivé.

"THE luckiest musical composition ever promulgated," Carlyle calls the Marseillaise. And the German poet, Klopstock, said more when on one occasion he said to its author, Rouget de L'Isle: "You lost us 30,000 Germans." The Germans, in fact, think so well of the Marseillaise that they have always claimed that the tune at least was "made in Germany."

But we who have never heard the Marseillaise when "the blood runs" and the "flag is in danger," apparently have never heard it at all. It may be we Americans do not know our Star Spangled Banner either, since few of us have ever heard it when more than its top notes were in danger.

It was after some particularly violent fighting, when "the river was as red as the soldiers' breeches," that a young French gunner, unnamed, wrote the description which is quoted by M. Victor Giraud, author of "La troisième France," published by the Librairie Hachette in Paris.

(*The Marseillaise Letter of a Gunner*)

Where we were, by the light of the firing, we could see the battlefield very distinctly, and never shall I see anything more fantastic than the thousands of red legs, in close rank, that charged; the gray legs commenced to tremble (they do not like the bayonet); the Marseillaise kept on, and the bugles sounded the charge, and our cannons kept on spitting. Finally, our infantry closed with the enemy. Not a gun shot; the bayonet — Suddenly, the call to charge stopped. The bugles called "to the Flag!" Instinctively we stopped firing, startled. The Marseillaise grew louder, and over there, further on, the call to the Flag continued. A dead silence — only the Marseillaise and the bugle; and we could make out the terrible conflict — suddenly the bugle stopped a second time, then at full blast they sounded the charge. The flag was recaptured. An immense uproar! Our guns replied all alone, and the Boches that night had to fly as fast as their legs could carry them. You who think you know the Marseillaise because you have heard it played at some prize-distribution, get rid of your illusion. To know it, it is necessary to have heard it as I have just described it to you, when the blood runs, and the flag is in danger.

"Lettres du Front," par Victor Giraud. Revue des Deux Mondes.

DONALD HANKEY

Donald Hankey, the author of "A Student in Arms," one of the most popular of the war books, is an Englishman, who was killed in action on the western front in October, 1916. He wrote his letters originally for the *London Spectator*. Mr. Strachey, editor of the *Spectator,* says that after reading the book you cannot get away from the conclusion that man, after all, is a noble animal; which is contrary to the pacifist assumption, just a little insulting, that all men are driven to war as to shambles, and are necessarily brutalized by fighting for a good cause.

Donald Hankey was chiefly interested in the great democratic experiment of the war, and its lasting and beneficial results after the war is over. He writes with mixed humor and seriousness and always with a warm kindliness. He writes with as much affection of "The Cockney Warrior" as of "The Beloved Captain," who was not a democrat at all, but rather a "justification of aristocracy." On the whole, he reserves his best sympathy for the Cockney. It takes more heroism for the Cockney to be a hero than for the Beloved Captain. Tell an English public school boy of some perilous adventure and he will thrill to it and say, "How jolly!" Tell the same thing to a boy in the East End of London and he will say: "Ow, I'm glad I weren't there!"

But when he has been "there" he has generally been ready. "A Student in Arms" is a fine tribute to the Englishman in arms, from whatever rank.

(Letter of Donald Hankey)

For every Englishman who philosophizes, there are a hundred who don't. For every soldier who prays, there are a thousand who don't. But there is hardly a man who will not return from the war bigger than when he left home. His language may have deteriorated. His "views" on religion and morals may have remained unchanged. He may be rougher in manner. But it will not be for nothing that he has learnt to endure hardship without making a song about it, that he has risked his life for righteousness' sake, that he has bound up the wounds of his mates, and shared with them his meager rations. We who have served in the ranks of "the first hundred thousand" will want to remember something more than the ingloriousness of war. We shall want to remember how adversity made men unselfish, and pain found them tender, and danger found them brave, and loyalty made them heroic. The fighting man is a very ordinary person; that's granted; but he has shown that the ordinary person can rise to unexpected heights of generosity and self-sacrifice.

Taken by permission from "A Student in Arms," by Donald Hankey. Published by E. P. Dutton & Co.

FRENCH SCHOOL BOY

French boys, fine of face, raised by your mothers,
Who from babyhood had slow and serious growth
In your large houses enclosed in leafy gardens.
Boys religious as I was, from childhood taught
To assist the priest and help in conducting the mass;
Older, you left intelligent mother and wise father
And came to complete in Paris the growth of your spirit.
You have sense and pleasing manners, politeness and warmth;
Latin and geometry you knew, and combining
Things respected from childhood and those learned in college,
Religious boys, much troubled by your studies,
At twenty years strangely you try to reconcile
Old beliefs with your new uncertainty.
— HENRI FRANCK, quoted in " Young France and New America," by Pierre de Lanux.

THE "défendre Maman" letter is written by a French schoolboy to the head of his school. It is characteristically French, in the charming intimacy it reveals, existing between the "Cher Monsieur l'Abbé" and his pupil, in its ardent and high spirit, and above all in its pretty Gallic conceit of "defending Mamma."

(*Letter of French Schoolboy*)

Cher Monsieur l'Abbé:
Listen to this! I offer myself as an English-

German interpreter the second day of the war. Knowing how to shoot, to ride horseback, and the bicycle and motorcycle, and to drive a car, and do fifty kilometers on foot if necessary, I expect to be accepted; they refuse me for lack of place. They have enough to do with the mobilization, it seems.

Commines being in danger, I take Mamma to England, as well as my little sister. On my return, here am I stuck!— You see I should like so much to go to the war. I would like to have offered myself a second time. Perhaps they would have taken me. Jean is at Saint-Astier, where he is in training, and I do nothing! Once getting into a company, I could have asked to go to the front. It would be so fine to make one of those bayonet charges that the Germans fear so much, and if necessary to die — at nineteen — for France!

If I do not get in the war, I would never dare to show myself again at the school. What would my friends say on learning that I had not shared the danger, that I have not rushed to "defend Mamma," as Regnault said in '70. Oh! how I envy those who fight, who are wounded, who die! Why in the devil didn't they accept me at once?

— Cited by "Les Roches" School.

"La France au-dessus de tout." Lettres de Combattants rassemblées et précedées d'une introduction par Raoul Narsy, rédacteur au Journal des Débats. Paris: Bloud et Gay.

WILLIAM M. BARBER

In the log book, as it is called, of the American Ambulance service, is a letter written by William M. Barber, of Toledo, Ohio, who went to France in May, 1916, and was wounded and received the Médaille Militaire. His letter is, we may flatter ourselves, characteristically American. It is boyish and enthusiastic. Everything is fine. Every one is wonderful. The ambulance driver is " a great boy." The doctors and the hospital are the best in the world. He is very happy, and his " spirits are high too "— as we may well believe:

(*Letter of William M. Barber*)

France, June 30, 1916.

Dearest " folks at home," abroad — and Grandma!

. . . My three soldiers were killed. I was hurt only a little. I am not disfigured in any way. It just tore my side and legs a bit.

The French treated me wonderfully. I succeeded in getting the next American Ambulance driven by Wheeler (a great boy) who took me to the city of ——, where our poste is. Here I was given first aid, and the Médecin Chef personally conducted me in an American Ambulance, in the middle of the night, to a very good hospital. They say I have the best doctor in France, in Paris.

Well, I woke up the next day in bed, and have been recuperating ever since. Every one is wonderful to me. General Pétain, second to Joffre, has stopped in to shake hands with me, and congratulate me, too, for above my bed hangs the Médaille Militaire, the greatest honor the French can give any one. Really, I am proud, although I don't deserve it any more than the rest. Please excuse my egotism.

Mr. Hill and my French lieutenant come to see me every day, and some of the boys also. They joke around here, saying that I am getting so well that they have lost interest in me and must move on. In three or four days I go to the hospital at Neuilly, where I can have every comfort.

Of course, you won't worry about me. I will be just as good as new soon, and really this is true.

The Germans peppered the life out of my car. No one goes on the road in the daylight, but the fellows brought me back the next day a handful of bullets taken from it, and said they could get me a bushel more if I desired them.

. . . For three days I was not allowed to eat or drink and could hardly move in bed. My spirits were high, too. I will try to write better and take more pains. . . .

. . . Well, here I am at Neuilly. This is a wonderful hospital, and they do treat you great! The doctors are the best in the world. I am very happy here and hope every day that you are as happy and never worry about me. I surely have given you a lot of trouble and anxiety. . . . The best of my experience is that I never once regretted the great trip, and I think I have done a small part of a great work, and my Médaille shows what the French think of my services. . . .

Good-by,

WILLIAM.

Taken by permission from "Friends of France." Published by Houghton Mifflin & Co.

VIVE L'ALSACE!

SOME young soldiers fight for "Maman," and others for grandmother and grandfather. The latter are the descendants of the 500,000 exiles from Alsace and Lorraine. The cynical Bismarck said he did not take the provinces for their beaux yeux alone. But it is of the beaux yeux of the fair land that the young French crusaders seem to think, more than of any ore deposits; it is to avenge grandmother and grandfather, and to win back for Maman her lost patrie. The following anonymous letter is quoted by M. Ernest Daudet:

("Vive l'Alsace" Letter)

My little mother:

I am writing to you again to ask for news of you. I have already written to you, but I do not know if you have received my letter. I am glad to have had a little rest to recover my strength. For we are departing for ——. I am going to see again my native village, tread the soil of my second country. I shall avenge grandmother and grandfather, and I shall kill as many Prussians as possible. I have already killed my share, but it is not yet enough. Finally, it is necessary to hope that our dear Alsace, your country, will return to us, and that it is I, your son, who will contribute a little towards its recovery.

I have already had many comrades, true friends, killed at my side. I have only been wounded in the arm. I am lucky. I have absolute confidence that I shall see you again, for I have a lucky star that shines over me.

Little mother, do not worry. If you could only hear how the cannon thunder! One sings in order to deaden the dreadful noise. Never has my tenor voice served me so well. At the sound of the charge, there are no longer men; there are specters. Half fall dead with their horses. One mounts the other horses, and it is all the time like that. The firing is terrible, but one pays no attention to it. In the morning, one is a brother in arms; in the evening, one mounts the phantoms in order to rush upon the enemy. Finally, have confidence, and in a near victory. And vive la France! And vive l'Alsace! which will soon be French.

"L'Âme française et allemande" Introduction par M. Ernest Daudet. Paris: Attinger Frères.

MAURICE GÉNEVOIX

MAURICE GÉNEVOIX was a second-year student in the École Normale in Paris in 1914. He had just completed a "study on Maupassant," and was looking forward to his holidays. Within a month, he was at the front, and had received his baptism of fire in the Battle of the Marne. His day by day record of his experiences gives a vivid, impressionistic, cinematographic picture of modern warfare. The author of "Under Fire" might have gone to his young countryman for some of his masterly pages; but hardly for the human, kindly portrait of the poilu.

(Letter of Maurice Génevoix)

Several times I walked up and down, passing and repassing soldiers still hustling one another in their endeavors to read the announcements. Strangely alike in appearance were they. The faces of one and all were mud-stained and bristles filled the hollows of their cheeks. Their blue great-coats bore traces of the dust of the road, of the mud of the fields, of the heavy rain; their boots and gaiters had long since acquired a permanently somber color; their clothes were worn and torn, at knees and elbows, and from their tattered sleeves protruded hands incredibly dirty and hardened. Most of them appeared wearied and wretched beyond description. Nevertheless, these were the men who had just fought with superhuman energy, who had proved themselves stronger than German bullets and bayonets; these men were the conquerors. . . .

To-morrow perhaps they must once again take up their knapsacks, and go marching for hours, despite feet that swell and burn; sleep beside ditches full of water, eating only when occasion presents, knowing hunger sometimes and thirst and coldness. They will go on, and among them not one will be found to grumble at the life before them. And when the hour sounds to fight once again, they will shoulder their rifles with the same easy indifference, will rush forward as eagerly between the bursts of enemy fire, will display the same tenacity before the mightiest efforts of the enemy. For in them dwell souls, ever scornful of weakness, strengthened and fortified by the conviction of victory, capable of conquering physical pain and weariness. Oh, all of you, my brothers in arms, we are going to do still better than we have already done, are we not?

" 'Neath Verdun," by Maurice Génevoix, with a preface by Ernest Lavisse. Translated by H. Grahame Richards. London: Hutchinson & Co.

R. DERBY HOLMES

CORPORAL R. DERBY HOLMES is a Yankee. He enlisted with the British army early in 1916. He went over on a horse boat. He saw some hard fighting, had some harrowing experiences, and received his Blighty. But all the suffering and all the experiences are as nothing, he says, compared with " the satisfaction of having done a bit in the great and just cause."

Corporal Holmes describes one of the ugliest incidents of the war, an incident which is said to explain the particular ferocity of the Canadians. Most stories of crucifixions are second-hand. But this Yankee's is direct. He prefaces his story by telling of a Canadian he encountered one night when crawling around on patrol in No Man's Land. They lay together in the mud for a time and compared notes, and then parted — each returning (supposedly) to his own trench. A little later, however, Corporal Holmes saw the Canadians going over their top. There had been no preliminary barrage and apparently no order to charge:

(Letter of R. Derby Holmes)

Well, there they were, going over, as many as two hundred of them — growling. . . . They swept across No Man's Land and into the Boche trench. There was the deuce of a ruckus over there for maybe two minutes, and then back they came — carrying something. Strangely enough there had been no machine-gun fire turned on them as they crossed, nor was there as they returned. They had cleaned that German trench! And they brought back the body of a man — nailed to a rude crucifix. The thing was more like a T than a cross. It was made of planks, perhaps two by five, and the man was spiked on by his hands and feet. Across the abdomen he was riddled with bullets, and again with another row higher up nearer his chest. The man was the sergeant I had talked to earlier in the night. What had happened was this: He had, no doubt, been taken by a German patrol. Probably he had refused to answer questions. Perhaps he had insulted an officer. They had crucified him and held him up above the parapet. With the first light his own comrades had naturally opened up on the thing with the Lewises, not knowing what it was. When it got lighter, and they recognized the hellish thing that had been done to one of their men, they went over. Nothing in the world could have stopped them. . . .

The Canadians were reprimanded for going over without orders. But they were not punished. For their officers went with them — led them.

Taken by permission from "A Yankee in the Trenches," by R. Derby Holmes. Published by Little, Brown & Co.

ALEXANDER McCLINTOCK

ALEXANDER MCCLINTOCK has a Distinguished Conduct Medal. The English King visited the American in the hospital and thanked him personally for his part in the engagement on the Somme, which left him with twenty-two pieces of shrapnel in his leg. For a time it looked as if he would not be able to give one interpretation to R. I. P.— rise if possible.

Alexander McClintock is a Kentuckian, and at one time was a ball player, and turned to bombs naturally and even affectionately, and he fought with the Canadians in Flanders — a combination hard to beat. After the third fight at Ypres, when forty per cent. of the Canadians were wiped out, and there was a call for three hundred volunteers, Mr. McClintock and a comrade started for headquarters. They expected to be received with applause, as he mock-heroically says, and to be praised for their bravery. But they couldn't even get near enough to hand in their names: " The whole battalion had gone ahead of us. That was the spirit of the Canadians."

(Letter of Alexander McClintock)

I was informed before my departure (from England) that a commission as lieutenant in the Canadian forces awaited my return from furlough, and I had every intention of going back to accept it. But since I got to America, things have happened. Now it's the army of Uncle Sam for mine. It's going to be a tough game, and a bloody one, and a sorrowful one for many. But it's up to us to save the issue where it's mostly right on one side and all wrong on the other — and I'm glad we're in. I'm not willing to quit soldiering now, but will be when we get through with this. When we finish up with this, there won't be any necessity for soldiering. The world will be free of war for a long, long time — and a God's mercy, that.

Taken by permission from "Best o' Luck," by Alexander McClintock. Published by George H. Doran Company.

ROBERT REASER

ROBERT REASER, the son of an artist, was himself studying art in New York, when he joined the ambulance unit formed by the City Club of New York, and sailed for France, in July, 1917. Robert is nineteen. He is tall. It is not easy for him to hide in shell-holes, and "scared" as he is, he says he cannot help "laughing at the way I am imitating that well known bird that sticks its head in the sand and feels hidden."

Just before leaving for the front, Robert wrote to his parents: "By to-morrow or the next day, at least, I expect we shall be at the place we started for just three months ago yesterday. You can imagine there is a good deal of conjecture as to what things will be like, and, of course, we are all laughing and 'kidding' each other, and wondering how we shall conduct ourselves under fire. J—— says that on the day after the first shell bursts near the convoy, the newspaper of some town in the south of France will have the report: 'A number of ambulances were reported to have passed through the city at 5:15 this morning, traveling south. Three wheels are known to have been touching the ground.'"

But it is not long before Robert is sending word that "Little Brother is having the time of his life!

I'm actually reveling in driving a bucking Ford over the worst shell-swept roads in France, and I guess I'm doing it as well as the rest of the crowd." (He has been cited for bravery.) In one of his letters Robert describes the roads:

(Letter of Robert Reaser)

... All this time the look of the country was changing, from the somewhat green fields and shattered buildings, gradually to the most utterly desolate stretches of ground that I have ever laid eyes on. ... The roads wind up and down over small hills which are moderately steep and whose tops are several hundred yards apart, sometimes half a mile. And on these hills there is absolutely nothing visible except upturned earth and rocks, the latter all shattered to tiny pieces — no stumps of trees even to break the monotony, and a good share of the time not a living thing visible except hundreds of rats scampering around over the road. It reminds me of the heaps of ashes I've seen after big fires, without any of the ruins. Of course, on closer view, remains of wagons and guns and all the things used in making war (even to horses and men) are scattered around and mixed in with the churned up earth. On bright days the middle distances look like the pictures of Arizona and New Mexico deserts; the same coloring and shapes in the hills. It is always picturesque and romantic, and only gruesome when you stop to think (which I do as little as possible), or when you have to pass an occasional disagreeable obstruction in the road.

Communicated.

ARTHUR GUY EMPEY

SERGEANT ARTHUR GUY EMPEY confesses that while he was serving with the British army he was more than once punished, put on the Crime Sheet as it is called, and generally for "Yankee impudence." When he first went over to London, and a British recruiting officer hailed him: "I s'y, myte, want to tyke on?" his reply was that he didn't know what it was, but he rather thought he would take a chance at it. And he did. He had eighteen months of it, and there were many times when he wished he were safe home again, in the little old town back of the Statue of Liberty, in Jersey no less. But he saw it through, and then with his blighty came back and told us all about it.

There are doubtless some who think that this "impudent Yankee" invented "Over the Top." At least he made it a familiar household phrase in America; a phrase that even the cats of the country came to know, as Mark Twain said of "Du bist wie eine Blume." Sergeant Empey also wrote a Tommy's dictionary, from as original a slant as Dr. Sam Johnson's when he defined oats as a food for horses and Scotchmen. Many of us were first initiated by Empey into the mysteries of "cooties" and "blighty" and "dixies" (which must be cleaned with mud!) and much besides; that V. C., for example, stands for "very careless" (with his life), and R. I. P. for "rest in pieces."

Sergeant Empey was responsible for a lot of Americans taking a chance at it, and going "over the top," if not actually, at least with their money and flaming sympathies. His message is earnest:

(*Letter of Arthur Guy Empey*)

After my discharge, and after a stormy trip across the Atlantic, one momentous day, in the haze of the early dawn I saw the Statue of Liberty looming over the port rail, and I wondered if ever again I would go "over the top with the best of luck and give them hell."

And even then, though it may seem strange, I was really sorry not to be back in the trenches with my mates. War is not a pink tea, but in a worth while cause like ours, mud, rats, cooties, shells, wounds, or death itself, are far outweighed by the deep sense of satisfaction felt by the man who does his bit.

There is one thing which my experience taught me that might help the boy who may have to go. It is this — anticipation is far worse than realization. In civil life a man stands in awe of the man above him, wonders how he could ever fill his job. When the time comes he rises to the occasion, is up and at it, and is surprised to find how much more easily than he anticipated he fills his responsibilities. It is really so " out there."

He has nerve for the hardships; the interest of the work grips him; he finds relief in the fun and comradeship of the trenches, and wins that best sort of happiness that comes with duty done.

Taken by permission from "Over the Top," by Arthur Guy Empey. Published by G. P. Putnam's Sons.

"THE GOOD SOLDIER"

M. Victor Giraud quotes the following letter. It was written by a young instructor to his father before going into an attack in which he lost his life. His name is Milavieille. Wherever the names of these heroes are known, they should be written down. The letter expresses the spirit of "the good soldier," Alan Seeger's "good soldier," for whom death holds no terrors. The letter also expresses simply and movingly the intimate and friendly relations existing between the officers and men, especially in the French army; between "my general" and his "children."

(Letter of " The Good Soldier")

The general arrived this morning. He spoke to our men. Against all discipline, our soldiers applauded him: "Bravo! my general! We'll get them, my general! You can depend upon us!" The general, with wet eyes, went away stammering: "Au revoir, my children! Thank you, my children!" I had tears in my eyes. Oh! it is fine, it is beautiful! And I think that he will be satisfied with us, our general.

Our men, in spite of forty days of the greatest

strain, have a superb morale. Father, I am calm. Before going into action, I shall have complete control of myself. If I fall, you can be tranquil; I shall have had the death of a good soldier and you can think of me with a serene spirit. If I fall, I shall fall facing them, without complaint, in full consciousness of my strength, of the clearness of my mind, of my free will. The war that we are fighting is worth dying for.

"Lettres du Front," par Victor Giraud. Revue des Deux Mondes.

"PAGES ACTUELLES" FROM THE FRENCH,

With two "current events" from American newspapers

(Letter of a French mother)

Sir: Thank you most sincerely for the letter that you have been good enough to write me. Thanks especially for the pains you have taken to tell me with so much delicate consideration the terrible news which crushes me. . . .

In this dreadful calamity, one great consolation is left to me. For seventeen years, I have fought for my son's life through all sorts of illnesses. I was able to rescue him from death only by the most constant care. I am very proud to have succeeded in saving his life, in order to permit him to die for his country. This is my great consolation.

— Printed in the *Paris Temps*.

(Letter of an American mother)

Allow me, as one who has lived until now an old woman, to express to you my thanks and appreciation for your many courtesies to me as mother of

Sergeant-Major William B. Jenkins. I had hoped my boy would get his chance in France, but it was not to be, so I am as submissive to his death as if he had died in the trenches in Europe.

Please accept my thanks for all your kindness and to any of his comrades that were with him in his sickness. With a sad heart I dictate these lines, but with a quickening pulse and an accelerated being I look forward to the day when victory shall come to the brave boys who are giving their lives for our beloved land. I shall ever love a soldier boy. May God's blessing be on you!

— Posted at Camp Upton, training camp at Yaphank, New York.

(Farewell of a French Soldier)

Dear god-father and god-mother:

I write to you in order not to kill mother whom a similar blow would surprise too much.

I was wounded September 29 at Saint-Hilaire-le-Grand. I have two hideous wounds, and I shall not last very long. They do not even conceal it from me.

I go without regret, with the consciousness of having done my duty.

Advise my parents, then, the best way you know how; tell them not to try to come to Suippes, they surely would not be in time.

Adieu, dear god-father, dear god-mother, dear parents, dear cousins, all you whom I loved.

Vive la France!

L. Bouny.
— Printed in the *Paris Temps.*

(Farewell of an American Soldier)

Mother dear, as we are all ready to go, just waiting for the word to set us in motion, your old pal wants to say adios to you alone.

We have been good pals, and have liked the same things, and now for the time being we are separated, but, mother dear, it will only be for a little while and I will be back with you again.

I will try to be a credit to you, I will never be a coward to bring disgrace to you.

Good-by, mother. God keep you safe.

"Mick" McHenry.
— Printed in the *Des Moines, Iowa, Register and Leader.*

"La France au-dessus de tout." Lettres de Combattants rassemblées et précedées d'une introduction par Raoul Narsy, rédacteur au Journal des Débats. Paris: Bloud et Gay.

A LAMENT

We who are left, how shall we look again
Happily on the sun, or feel the rain,
Without remembering how they who went
Ungrudgingly, and spent
Their all for us, loved, too, the sun and rain?
A bird among the rain-wet lilac sings —
But we, how shall we turn to little things
And listen to the birds and winds and streams
Made holy by their dreams,
Nor feel the heart-break in the heart of things?
— WILFRID GIBSON.

THE END

PRINTED IN THE UNITED STATES OF AMERICA

THE following pages contain advertisements of a few of the Macmillan books on kindred subjects.

By JULIEN H. BRYAN

Illustrated. Cloth, 12mo.

Here we have the story of the experiences of a Princeton Junior—a boy of seventeen, who went to the war and drove an ambulance car in the Verdun and Champagne sectors. He tells exactly what he saw and heard in the American Ambulance Corps, bringing his story down to August, 1917. His accounts are modest, interesting, sometimes amusing—always vivid.

War books by soldiers are very popular these days. The author-fighter has contributed some of the most informing volumes that have been issued on the great conflict. Of all of those who have been to the front and have returned to write about it, no one, perhaps, has had more unusual experiences than fell to the lot of this youth. He has written a book in which he tells what happened to him and his immediate associates; a book that is remarkable for the thrilling character of its narrative, the spirit of good humor, of adventure and excitement which runs through it.

Mr Bryan had his kodak with him and his text is illustrated with many altogether unusual pictures, giving a new and clear idea as to the war and its method of prosecution.

THE MACMILLAN COMPANY

EDWARD G. D. LIVEING

With an Introduction by John Masefield

"The Attack," says Mr. Masefield in his introduction, "on the fortified village of Gommecourt, which Mr. Liveing describes in these pages with such power and color, was a part of the first great allied attack on July 1st, 1916, which began the Battle of the Somme. . . .

"Mr. Liveing's story is very well told. It is a simple and most vivid account of a modern battle. No better account has been written in England since the war began. I hope that so rare a talent for narrative may be recognized. I hope, too, that Mr. Liveing may soon be able to give us more stories as full of life as these."

THE MACMILLAN COMPANY

MASEFIELD'S NEW WAR BOOK

The Old Front Line

By JOHN MASEFIELD

Illustrated. Cloth, 12mo. $1.00

What Mr. Masefield did for the Gallipoli Campaign, he now does for the Campaign in France. His subject is the old front line as it was when the battle of the Somme began. His account is vivid and gripping—a huge conflict seen through the eyes of a great poet, this is the book.

Of the importance of the battle, Mr. Masefield writes:

"The old front line was the base from which the battle proceeded. It was the starting place. The thing began there. It was the biggest battle in which our people were ever engaged, and so far it has led to bigger results than any battle of this war since the Battle of the Marne. It caused a great falling back of the enemy armies. It freed a great tract of France, seventy miles long, by from ten to twenty-five miles broad. It first gave the enemy the knowledge that he was beaten."

THE MACMILLAN COMPANY
Publishers   64-66 Fifth Avenue   New York

Illustrated, Cloth, $1.25

High courage, deep sympathy without sentimentality, and an all-saving sense of humor amid dreadful and depressing conditions are the salient features of this little book. The author, who preserves her anonymity, has been "over the top" in the fullest sense. She has faced bombardments and aerial raids, she has calmly removed her charges under fire, she has tended the wounded and dying amid scenes of carnage and confusion, and she has created order and comfort where but a short time before all was chaos and suffering. And all the while she marvels at the uncomplaining fortitude of others, never counting her own. Many unusual experiences have befallen this "war nurse" and she writes of them all in a gripping, vivid fashion.

THE MACMILLAN COMPANY

LIBRARY OF CONGRESS

0 007 691 423 0